Waiting in Exile

Gregory Paul

Copyright © 2025 by Gregory Paul

All rights reserved. No part of this publication may be reproduced, distributed, or transmitted in any form or by any means, including photocopying, recording, or other electronic or mechanical methods, without the prior written permission of the publisher, except in the case of brief quotations embodied in critical reviews and certain other noncommercial uses permitted by copyright law.

This is a work of fiction. Names, characters, places, and incidents either are the product of the author's imagination or are used fictitiously. Any resemblance to actual persons, living or dead, events, or locales is entirely coincidental.

Published by Donahue Publishing

First Edition

ISBN: 979-8-89864-022-4

For information about special discounts for bulk purchases, please contact Donahue Publishing at info@donahuepublishing.co.

www.donahuepublishing.co

Contents

Foreword 1

Chapter One: Before Judy 3

Chapter Two: Slipping Again 7

Chapter Three: Building a Family 12

Chapter Four: Secrets in the Silence 19

Chapter Five: Calm Before the Storm 26

Chapter Six: The Raid 33

Chapter Seven: The Fallout 45

Chapter Eight: Cage Life 55

Chapter Nine: The Second Sentence 65

Chapter Ten: The Lie Detector 73

Chapter Eleven: The Unseen Sentence 83

Chapter Twelve: Manufactured Monsters 92

Chapter Thirteen: The Breaking Point 100

Chapter Fourteen: Rogers Roost 106

Chapter Fifteen: Breaking the Cycle 114

Chapter Sixteen: Angie's Smile and the Echoes of Trying 121

Chapter Seventeen: The Fire Still Burns 129

Chapter Eighteen: Forged in Fire 140

Chapter Nineteen: Triggered 148

Chapter Twenty: The Long Climb 158

Chapter Twenty-One: A Light Through the Cracks 167

Gregory Paul

Foreword

This book is not an easy read, nor was it an easy life to live. It's a testament to survival—to holding on by the thinnest of threads when everything and everyone seems designed to push you off the edge.

I wrote this not for sympathy, but for truth. There are people behind headlines. There are stories behind labels. I was one of those people. I still am.

In 2009, my life imploded in a single night. A multi-agency raid turned my home into a crime scene. They found three video files on my computer—files I had stumbled across years earlier, buried in massive download bundles. I never sought them out. I never shared them. But they were there. I did what I thought was right—I told the truth. I admitted they existed. That honesty became the prosecution's entire case.

Within months, I lost everything: my job, my home, my reputation, my future. But the loss that destroyed me wasn't any of those things. It was my daughter, Jenna—the little girl who used to fall asleep on my chest, who sang with me until we couldn't breathe from laughing. The system didn't just punish me. It erased me. It branded me with a label that follows me everywhere, telling the world I'm a monster, regardless of context, regardless of truth, regardless of the person I actually am.

I spent a year in jail. Five years on probation. And now, a lifetime on a registry with no path to redemption. No matter how much I change, how much I grow, how much I prove myself—I will die with this label. The system offers no mechanism for mercy. It wasn't designed to rehabilitate. It was designed to erase.

But I refused to be erased.

This book is my act of defiance. It's my refusal to let their narrative become my truth. It's my voice, raised from exile, speaking to anyone who will listen. To other fathers who have lost their children. To people living in basements because no one will rent to them. To anyone who has been reduced to a headline, a statistic, a checkbox on a form.

I'm not asking you to agree with everything I say. I'm not asking for your approval or your forgiveness. I'm asking for something simpler and harder: your attention. Your willingness to see beyond the label. Your capacity to consider that maybe—just maybe—the system that claims to protect us sometimes destroys innocent lives in the process.

This is my story. The whole story. The parts that hurt to write and the parts that hurt even more to remember. The moments of shame and the moments of defiant hope. The truth about what it's like to be permanently punished for a mistake, to lose your child to a system that offers no appeals, to survive when survival feels like the cruelest option.

If you're reading this and you've ever felt completely alone, ever felt like the world has decided who you are without knowing your truth, ever wondered if you can survive the unsurvivable—you're not alone.

I'm here. And I'm still standing.

Let this be a voice for the voiceless. Let this be light where there was once only shadow.

Gregory Paul

Chapter One: Before Judy

Before all of this—before the labels, the courtrooms, the lost years—I was just a guy trying to make sense of fatherhood. A single dad in his thirties, working hard and loving harder. My world revolved around one little girl with wide eyes and a firecracker laugh: Jenna, my daughter, my joy, my reason for breathing.

I had no idea that everything I was building—everything we were building together—was about to be ripped apart by a system that would brand me guilty before I ever stepped foot in a courtroom. But that's getting ahead of myself.

This is the story of before. Before I became a number on a registry. Before I learned what it means to be permanently exiled from your own life. This is about when I still believed that being a good father was enough protection against the world's capacity for destruction.

I worked at Red Lobster in Rochester Hills, Michigan. It wasn't glamorous, but it paid the bills and gave me structure. I was a manager there, the guy with the clipboard and the ready smile, making sure the team was running smoothly, the guests were happy, and the kitchen didn't implode. I was good at it. Organized. Charismatic. Even a little too passionate at times.

But work was just the background music. The real show started the second I walked through my apartment door and saw Jenna's face light up.

She was around six or seven at the time, and already had this old soul wrapped in a child's body. She'd ask big questions, draw pictures with tiny details, and crawl up onto my lap like it was still her throne. I'd cook us dinner—usually something quick and cheesy—and we'd sit down to eat like it was a ritual. She always asked if we could watch Disney's Tarzan after. Always.

Those dinners were sacred to me. Jenna would tell me about her day at school, acting out conversations with her teacher, mimicking her classmates with perfect comedic timing. I'd watch her face animated in the kitchen light and think: This is it. This is what I'm fighting to stay sober for. This moment, this laugh, this little person who thinks I hung the moon.

Her bedroom was her palace. I had rigged up a dome tent inside her room and set up a little air mattress inside it. The walls were covered in Blue's Clues, Toy Story, and The Lion King stickers. There were glow-in-the-dark stars on the ceiling, and we'd lie there for hours just staring up, talking about anything and everything. Dinosaurs. The moon. Her classmates. God. I lived for those conversations.

"Dad," she said one night, her voice small in the darkness of her tent-palace, "do you think the stars can see us too?"

"I think they're watching over us," I told her, and meant it.

I had no way of knowing that soon, I'd be staring up at different stars through prison bars, wondering if she could see them too.

I wanted her to have what I had growing up: a sense of family, of being known, of being loved. My siblings and I were close growing up, and Jenna and her cousin, Kylie, had that same spark between them. Kylie was more reserved, more logical, while Jenna had this dramatic streak, all heart and passion. They were opposites, but they clicked like puzzle pieces.

Still, I knew something was missing.

Gregory Paul

I wanted Jenna to have more than just a great dad. I wanted her to have a family—a real family. A mom figure. Siblings. Laughter in the kitchen. Chaos in the living room. I was trying to fill the void that her mother had left, even though I couldn't admit that out loud yet.

And that's what led me to Rayna. That's what made me vulnerable to the woman who would destroy everything I'd built.

But let's not get ahead of ourselves.

Back then, I was trying to build something stable out of the wreckage of my own youth. I'd been through addiction, had battled alcohol more times than I could count. I wasn't perfect—hell, I was still figuring out how to stay sober—but I was fighting for something better. For her. For Jenna.

Every day sober was a victory I counted in Jenna's smiles. Every responsible decision was an investment in our future together. I went to meetings. I worked my program. I showed up. Because she was watching, and she deserved a father who was present, not just physically there.

I was the kind of guy who took notes during parent-teacher conferences and showed up to every dance recital. I'd braid her hair—badly—but she loved that I tried. She once told me, "Dad, you make the best mac and cheese in the world." And I believed her.

I still believe her.

I wasn't wealthy. I wasn't wise. But I was present.

And for a little while, that felt like enough.

But the system doesn't care if you're present. It doesn't care if you're fighting every day to be better. It doesn't care if you're somebody's entire world. Life has a way of testing your foundation right when you think it's strongest.

What I didn't know was that the cracks weren't in my foundation. The cracks were in a system that would take one woman's lies and turn them into my life sentence. The cracks were in a justice system that prioritizes conviction rates over truth.

But I'm getting ahead of myself again.

This is the story of before. When I still believed that love was protection enough. When I thought being a good father was a shield against injustice.

I was wrong about a lot of things back then.

But I wasn't wrong about loving Jenna.

Chapter Two: Slipping Again

The thing about recovery is that it teaches you to recognize the signs in others before you can identify them in yourself. I should have known. I should have seen what was coming.

But when you're desperate to build something—anything—that looks like a normal life, you'll ignore red flags that are practically screaming in your face.

Here's where it all started to fall apart again. I had been clinging to the idea that I could build something stable, something worth holding onto. But deep down, I was starting to get suspicious—about her, about myself, about whether anything I believed in was real.

Rayna had seemed like hope wrapped in pretty packaging. She understood addiction because she'd been there. She got why I went to meetings, why I counted days, why I sometimes stared at Jenna sleeping and wondered if I was strong enough to be the father she deserved. Or at least, that's what I told myself.

She said all the right things. "I'm clean now, too." "We can help each other stay sober." "Jenna needs a stable family." All the words I wanted to hear, delivered with the kind of conviction that only comes from someone who's had plenty of practice lying.

This one night stands out in my memory like a scar. I picked up Rayna after a late night at the restaurant. She'd been drinking, and so had I. We went back to my place, cracked a few more beers, turned on the TV, surfed the web, listened to music. It felt normal at first. But then she kept disappearing into the bathroom. Not once, not twice—over and over. Each time she'd be in there for fifteen or twenty minutes.

I knew what she was doing.

She was using my hand mirror to snort cocaine in my bathroom. I had seen it before. I knew the signs. And the worst part? I had been stupid enough to let myself believe she was clean.

The mirror I used to check my tie before parent-teacher conferences. The same bathroom where Jenna brushed her teeth every morning. The space I thought was safe, sacred even, and she was turning it into her personal drug den.

That's when it hit me: she wasn't just using it in my home. She was using me. The whole relationship, the promises, the talk about building a family together—it was all just another con to give her a place to get high.

I snapped.

I kicked her out of my house and drove her back to her place in Royal Oak. I was so angry, so disappointed, so tired. Then I drove all the way back home to 20 Mile Rd. and Schoenherr—fuming the entire ride.

The drive back felt like forty miles of reckoning. Every mile marker was another reality check I'd been avoiding. How had I let someone bring drugs into Jenna's home? How had I been so desperate for connection that I'd ignored every instinct screaming at me to run?

We made up the next week. Of course we did. She cried, told me she slipped, swore she'd never do it again. I wanted to believe her. Hell, I needed to believe her. That's the kind of man I was—always trying to fix someone, always trying to save a drowning soul when I barely had air in my own lungs.

"It was just a moment of weakness," she said, tears streaming down her face. "I've been clean for months. You know how hard this is. You know what it's like to slip."

And I did know. That's what made her manipulation so effective. She was using my own recovery against me, turning my empathy into her weapon. Every excuse she made was something I'd told myself at some point.

So the following weekend, I took my desktop computer over to her place. This was 2005, and I was proud of my plug-and-play setup. All I needed was a landline and an outlet. I had internet and power, and I was ready to roll.

She was hosting a small gathering at her house, a party with some of her old friends. I didn't know any of them, but I recognized the type. They were all already high when I arrived. The smell of cocaine and stale beer hung in the air.

I stayed anyway.

Looking back, I can't explain why I didn't turn around and leave the second I walked through that door. Maybe I was already too invested in the fantasy. Maybe I was scared of going back to being alone with just Jenna and me against the world. Maybe I was just tired of being the responsible one all the time.

I didn't use any. I was drinking, yeah, but I wasn't doing blow. Still, my sobriety was already shot to hell at that point. She pulled me aside after everyone left, curled up next to me on the couch, and in the most casual tone you could imagine, told me those guys had all been former Johns.

My stomach turned.

"Johns?" I said, even though I knew exactly what she meant.

"Clients," she said, like she was talking about the weather. "From before. When I was working."

Working. That's what she called it. Like prostitution was just another job she'd left behind, no different than quitting retail or restaurant work.

She wasn't just slipping—she had never stopped being that person. I realized, maybe too late, that I had fallen in love with a fantasy. She wasn't who she said she was.

The woman I thought I was building a life with didn't exist. The clean, reformed addict who wanted to help me create a stable home for Jenna? Pure fiction. I'd been dating a ghost, a carefully constructed lie designed to give her access to my home, my life, and my desperate need to believe in second chances.

I went home the next day and packed up my things. I left her behind without a backward glance. That was the end of Rayna.

At least, that's what I told myself.

But you can't just walk away from the damage that easily. The doubt she'd planted had already taken root. If I could be fooled that completely, that thoroughly, what did that say about my judgment? What did that say about my ability to protect Jenna from the world—or from my own poor choices?

But damage doesn't end when the person leaves the room. It lingers. It buries itself in your habits, your doubts, your fears. I had thought I was saving her. What I hadn't realized was that I was drowning too.

That relationship taught me something crucial: I didn't know how to protect myself. I didn't know when to walk away until the walls were already caving in. I mistook chaos for chemistry.

More than that, it taught me I was willing to compromise everything—my sobriety, my principles, my daughter's safety—for the illusion of not being alone. That's a dangerous realization for any parent, but especially for a single father trying to prove he's enough.

And somewhere in the wreckage of that relationship, a little voice inside me started to whisper something I didn't want to hear.

Maybe this is all you're good for—trying to fix broken people.

Maybe you're just as broken as they are.

Maybe Jenna deserves better than a father who can't tell the difference between love and desperation.

But that voice? I'd silence it soon enough. At least, I thought I would. Until the next storm rolled in.

What I didn't know was that the next storm wouldn't just test my judgment about women or addiction or my ability to stay sober. The next storm would test whether the system I'd always trusted to protect innocent people would recognize that I was one of them.

And I was about to find out that sometimes, the system doesn't care about truth. Sometimes it just needs someone to blame.

Chapter Three: Building a Family

I should have learned my lesson with Rayna. Should have recognized the pattern—the desperation, the red flags, the way I kept choosing chaos and calling it love. But when you're a single father trying to give your daughter the family you never had, sometimes you ignore every instinct that's screaming at you to run.

The truth is, I was terrified Jenna would grow up feeling incomplete, the way I had before my sister came along. I wanted her to have what I'd had—siblings, noise in the house, someone to share the burden of being a kid in an unpredictable world.

All I really ever wanted was a family of my own so I could bring up Jenna with some brothers and sisters like I had. Being an only child until six had felt like carrying a weight I couldn't name. I knew that all too well before the age of six. That's when Sherry, my little sister, was born. Then, later in life, I got my stepsisters. But Sherry was my favorite little troublemaker.

Sherry got it—the way family should feel. Protective but playful, loyal but not blind to each other's faults. I wanted Jenna to have that kind of bond, that built-in best friend who'd have her back no matter what.

By this time, she'd had her daughter, Kylie, which was perfect because she was only one year younger than Jenna. We had them play together all the time, and they grew up loving each other as cousins. Kylie was a holy terror! No fear, no filter, and no holds barred! Jenna, on the other hand, was reserved and introverted—but highly intelligent. She would go on to earn a full scholarship to Central Michigan for child psychology and business management.

Watching them together—Jenna's careful planning and Kylie's fearless chaos—reminded me why family mattered. They balanced each other. They made each other braver, smarter, and more complete. That's what I wanted to build for Jenna. A house full of that kind of love.

But I digress. At this point, Jenna was probably six or seven years old, and I was trying my hardest to find a woman to build a family with. Didn't matter if it was a blended family with stepkids or if I made some new kids of my own. I was up for anything with a good woman.

Looking back, I can see how desperate that sounds. How dangerous it was to be that open, that willing to accept any situation as long as it filled the quiet spaces in our apartment. But I'd convinced myself I was being practical, not reckless. I was being a good father, not a desperate man.

That's when I met Judy.

She had three kids crammed into a tiny two-bedroom apartment in Clawson, Michigan. They'd come up from Indiana about a year earlier, running from their past. It was chaos—but the kind of chaos I thought I could handle. Her girls were sweet, and her oldest daughter, Tiffany, became like a sister to Jenna. I figured, why not? This could work. We had an instant sort of chemistry. Judy had been through some stuff, sure, but who hadn't?

"Chemistry." That's what I called it when someone understood my damage without judging it. When they nodded at my stories about addiction and recovery, and didn't flinch. I mistook shared trauma for compatibility, broken recognizing broken for some kind of cosmic connection.

Waiting in Exile

Judy was pretty in a tired way, like someone who'd been beautiful before life wore her down. She had this laugh that made you want to protect her from whatever had made it so rare. And her kids—they were hungry for stability in a way that broke my heart. Tiffany would light up when I asked about her day. The younger girls would actually listen when I told them to clean up their toys.

It felt like I could fix this. Like I could be the father figure they needed and give Jenna the siblings she deserved. Win-win, right?

Then I found out her oldest son, Daniel, was in jail down in Indiana. They had him arrested in connection with the death of his stepfather. Her daughter, Christina, had stayed behind to raise her one-year-old baby. It was all... a bit much. But I was already in it. Hook, line, and sinker.

"In connection with the death." That's how she put it the first time she told me. Not "murder." Not "killed." Just "in connection with." Like he'd been nearby when something unfortunate happened, instead of being the one who pulled the trigger.

The way she talked about it made it sound like a misunderstanding. A case of being in the wrong place at the wrong time. Poor Daniel, caught up in something bigger than himself. I wanted to believe her version because the alternative meant I was falling for someone whose family was capable of things I didn't want to imagine.

I'd catch Judy doing cocaine and sneaking drinks when she thought nobody was watching. And I'd think to myself: Jesus, isn't this just like the last one? The broken ones. The ones who needed saving.

That was my type.

Captain Save-a-Ho. That's what I was.

Gregory Paul

The pattern was so obvious I should have been embarrassed. Find a woman with addiction issues, tell myself I could love her clean, ignore every red flag until it was too late to walk away without destroying something. Rinse and repeat.

But this felt different because of the kids. This wasn't just about me and my need to fix someone. This was about giving Jenna the family I'd promised her, even if I had to build it out of broken pieces.

I confronted her gently, tried to guide her back on track. She'd nod and agree, and for a while, it seemed like she wanted what I wanted: a stable home, a blended family, peace. But there was something always lurking just beneath her eyes—like her past was dragging her under.

Little did I know exactly how far down that past would reach.

"I'm trying, Greg," she'd say, tears in her eyes after I'd find another empty bottle hidden behind the laundry detergent. "I just need time. This thing with Daniel... it's got me so stressed. Once that's resolved, everything will be different."

Everything was always going to be different once something else was resolved. Once Daniel's case was settled. Once Christina moved up from Indiana. Once the lawyers stopped calling. There was always another crisis on the horizon that justified why she couldn't get clean right now.

Eventually, I got through to her. Things got better. They got so good, I decided to move us all into a four-bedroom townhouse just down the road in Clawson, right near my new job as assistant general manager at Applebee's. I felt like we were turning a corner. Jenna was being blended with Tiffany, Erica, and Courtney—like sisters. I'd cook big dinners, play music in the background, and try to recapture some sense of a normal life.

Those months were the closest I'd ever come to having the family I'd dreamed of. Jenna helping Tiffany with homework. The younger girls fighting over who got to sit next to me at dinner. Judy actually laughing without that haunted look in her eyes.

I thought we'd made it. I thought I'd finally built something that would last.

From time to time, Judy would have a lawyer over, and they'd sit at the kitchen table and talk for an hour or more in hushed tones. I asked her what was going on, and of course, I assumed it had something to do with Daniel's case.

"Just paperwork," she'd say when I asked. "You know how lawyers are. They make everything complicated."

I'd see them passing documents back and forth, Judy signing things with shaking hands. Sometimes she'd cry after the lawyer left. But when I tried to comfort her, she'd just say she was worried about Daniel and change the subject.

I should have pushed harder. Should have demanded to know what kind of "paperwork" required that many late-night meetings. But I was so invested in the fantasy of our blended family that I convinced myself it was better not to know.

Little did I know that she was about to become a defendant in that same case.

Conspiracy to commit murder.

That's what the State of Indiana was saying. Apparently, she was considered a person of interest in the murder of her second husband. Her son Daniel had pulled the trigger. Her daughter, Christina, hid the gun. There was motive. They wanted to cash in on a multi-million dollar life insurance policy and seize the profitable Kirby vacuum sales team and office down in Merrillville, Indiana.

Murder for money. That's what it came down to. Not passion, not self-defense, not even a moment of rage that got out of hand. Cold, calculated murder for an insurance payout and a vacuum cleaner business.

And the woman I'd been sharing a bed with, the woman I'd trusted with my daughter's safety—she was potentially the mastermind behind it all.

What the hell had I gotten myself into?

Out of the frying pan and into the fire. Jesus Christ, I thought Rayna was bad. But this? This was a new level of messed up. Is Judy guilty? I didn't want to believe it. I couldn't. I told myself she wasn't involved. Maybe Daniel did it himself. Maybe Christina was manipulated. Maybe Judy had no idea. That's the story I clung to, because the alternative was too much to bear.

The alternative meant I'd moved my daughter into a house with someone capable of orchestrating murder. It meant every gentle moment, every family dinner, every time I'd watched Judy tuck the girls into bed—all of it had been a performance by someone who could kill for money.

It meant my judgment wasn't just poor—it was dangerous.

And by then, I lived there. I was knee-deep. Her kids were calling me a father figure. I couldn't just walk away.

Or could I? That's the question that kept me up at night. Was I staying because those kids needed me, or because I was too proud to admit I'd been completely wrong about someone again? Was I protecting Jenna or putting her in more danger by staying?

So I stayed.

I stood by her. I tried to block out the whispers in my head. I tried to rationalize every red flag. Because when you're desperate to build a family, sometimes you're willing to light yourself on fire just to keep others warm.

I told myself I was being loyal. Noble, even. Standing by someone when they needed it most. But the truth was simpler and uglier: I was afraid of being alone again. Afraid of telling Jenna we had to go back to being just the two of us. Afraid of admitting that I'd chosen wrong again.

I won't lie to you. There were nights I'd lie in bed and stare at the ceiling, thinking: This isn't going to end well.

And I was right.

What I didn't know was that it would end worse than I could have imagined. That my loyalty to a woman who might be a murderer would be twisted into something it never was. That trying to be a good father to damaged kids would be used as evidence of my own guilt.

The system doesn't care about context. It doesn't care that you were trying to build a family for your daughter. It doesn't care that you believed in second chances.

All it cares about is finding someone to blame when the real monsters slip through the cracks.

Gregory Paul

Chapter Four: Secrets in the Silence

You know that feeling when you walk into a room and realize everyone was just talking about you? That's what living with Judy started to feel like—except the conversation was about murder, and I was the only one who didn't know it was happening.

The townhouse in Clawson looked like any other suburban dream from the outside. Four bedrooms, a little courtyard, a white front door with a wreath Judy picked out from a local craft store. Inside, it was organized chaos. Kids' shoes by the door, laundry in rotation, Judy yelling about someone not rinsing their plate. Normal, almost. There was a silence that crept in at night, after the dishes were done and the girls were asleep. That silence? It was hiding things.

Looking back, I can see that I was living in two different realities. There was the surface reality—family dinners, homework help, bedtime stories. Jenna finally had the siblings I'd always wanted for her, and I had the chaos of a full house that made me feel like I was doing something right.

Then there was the reality underneath—the one where every phone call made Judy jump, where certain topics made her eyes go dark, where she'd disappear into the bedroom for hours after the lawyer visits. I told myself the surface was real and the underneath was just trauma. But trauma and guilt can look exactly the same to someone who wants to believe.

Judy had a lawyer over again one Thursday night. They sat at the kitchen table while I kept the girls occupied in the living room. I couldn't hear much, but the tension?

Waiting in Exile

That I could feel. When I asked her what it was about, she gave me the usual: "It's about Daniel's case. Just some paperwork."

"Paperwork" was becoming Judy's favorite word. Daniel's paperwork. Indiana paperwork. Legal paperwork that required lawyers to come to our house at eight o'clock at night and speak in whispers that didn't sound like paperwork at all.

I'd catch fragments sometimes. "Grand jury." "Conspiracy charges." "Extradition." Words that made my stomach turn, even though I didn't fully understand why they were being said in my kitchen.

I wanted to believe her. I needed to. But it was all starting to feel like wet cement drying around my ankles.

The worst part wasn't the lies—it was how good she was at making me feel guilty for questioning them. "You don't trust me," she'd say when I pushed too hard. "After everything we've built together, you still think I'm lying to you?" And I'd find myself apologizing for being suspicious, like doubt was a character flaw instead of common sense.

The truth? Judy wasn't just worried about Daniel. She was worried about herself. She was being named a co-defendant in the murder of her second husband. The State of Indiana was ready to go after her for conspiracy to commit murder. And I was just a few feet away, folding laundry, completely in the dark.

Co-defendant. That word hit me like a physical blow when I finally learned what was really happening. Not "concerned mother." Not "worried about her son." Co-defendant in a murder conspiracy. Which meant the state believed she didn't just know about the murder—she helped plan it.

Gregory Paul

Judy had told me Daniel shot his stepdad in a moment of rage. She said the oldest daughter, Christina, helped cover it up. But now, according to the state, it was a setup. Cold. Calculated. They tried to make it look like an accident—twice. The first time, they poisoned him. Didn't work. There was money on the line. Her second husband had a massive life insurance policy and a booming Kirby vacuum sales office down in Merrillville, Indiana. The entire thing reeked.

And Judy? She'd been in the room during the planning.

Two attempts. That's what made it premeditated in the eyes of the law. The first attempt failed, so they regrouped and tried again. That's not a crime of passion—that's a business decision. And the business was murder.

The woman who made my daughter's lunch every morning, who helped with homework and insisted on family movie nights, had allegedly sat in a room and planned how to kill a man for money. The mind rejects information like that. It's too big, too impossible, too much like something that happens to other people.

My hands shook when I first found out. Not because I feared for my safety, but because I realized I had been living in a house of lies. I had treated these kids like my own. I helped pay their bills, cooked them dinner, tucked them in at night. I gave Judy everything I had emotionally. And she gave me secrets.

Worse than secrets—she gave me complicity. Because every day I stayed, every bill I helped pay, every family photo we took, made me more entangled in her web. The State of Indiana wouldn't care that I was innocent. They'd care if I was there. If I was involved. That I looked guilty by association.

Waiting in Exile

Worse yet, I started thinking back—back to the subtle things she'd say or do. Her reluctance to talk about Indiana. Her nervous energy when the lawyer called. The way she flinched when I asked about Christina. I had chalked it all up to trauma. Turns out, it was guilt.

I remember her getting a call once while we were all watching TV. She answered it, listened for about thirty seconds, then hung up without saying a word. When I asked who it was, she said, "Wrong number." But her hands were shaking as she put the phone down.

"Wrong number" calls don't make you shake. Calls from prosecutors do.

And I was too blind to see it.

But I stayed. Why? Because of Jenna. Because of the girls. Because I had grown to love those damn kids like they were my own. And because, deep down, I still wanted to believe Judy was innocent. Maybe she got caught up in something. Maybe it was all circumstantial. Maybe love makes you stupid.

Or maybe desperation does. Because that's what it was—desperation to make this blended family work, no matter what the cost. I'd promised Jenna siblings. I'd promised myself I could build something stable. And I wasn't ready to admit that I'd built it on a foundation of murder and lies.

The kids didn't know much. Tiffany still asked me to help with her math homework. Erica still wanted me to read her bedtime stories. Courtney still climbed into my lap to watch cartoons. They were innocent in all this, and walking away would destroy them too.

How do you explain to a little girl that you can't be her stepdad anymore because her mother might be a killer?

I remember one night we sat out on the small back patio drinking a bottle of wine after the kids were in bed. The stars were out, and the cool fall air was just starting to bite. She looked over at me, her eyes glassy, and asked, "Do you think I'm a bad person?"

It came out of nowhere.

"No," I said. Too quickly.

She smiled a little. "Good. Because I'm not."

The way she said it—like she was trying to convince herself as much as me. Like she'd been practicing that line, testing it out to see if it sounded true.

"I never wanted anyone to get hurt," she said then, staring up at the stars. "You have to believe that."

But wanting and planning are two different things. And in that moment, sitting there in the dark, I knew she was guilty. I knew, and I stayed anyway.

Then she kissed me like that settled everything. But it didn't. I wiped my cheek.

There was a fire under the surface of this life we had built, and I was starting to feel the heat.

The fire was about to consume everything. And I was about to learn that when you're standing too close to someone else's flames, the system assumes you struck the match.

One afternoon, I saw Detective Skagnetti at a local middle school event. He was the same Clawson detective I'd occasionally see come into Applebee's. We'd known each other from around town, always cordial. But this time, he avoided eye contact. It was subtle, but it hit like a punch to the gut. I knew then that something was coming. I just didn't know how bad it would get.

Skagnetti had always been friendly before—the kind of cop who'd ask about the restaurant business and complain about his diet. But that day, he looked right through me like I was already wearing orange. Like he knew something I didn't know yet.

That's when I realized they weren't just investigating Judy. They were investigating everyone around her, including me.

Looking back now, I wonder how long the dominoes had been falling before I even realized I was standing in their path. Judy wasn't just a woman with a complicated past—she was actively hiding her involvement in a murder that would soon be national news. The kind of story that ends up on Dateline, Snapped, or A&E. And me? I was just trying to build a family. Just trying to be a dad.

But the system doesn't care about your intentions. It doesn't care that you were trying to give your daughter siblings or that you believed in second chances. It only cares about who was where when the crime happened, and who can be blamed when the public demands answers.

I was about to become a very convenient answer.

It wasn't just betrayal I felt. It was humiliation. Shame. The creeping realization that I was going to get caught in the blast radius of someone else's crime.

The shame was the worst part. Not just that I'd been fooled, but that I'd been fooled so completely. That I'd moved my innocent daughter into a house with someone capable of murder. That I'd been so desperate for family that I'd ignored every warning sign screaming at me to run.

But what could I do?

I was part of the story now—whether I liked it or not.

Part of the story. That's all anyone would see when this got out. Not the man trying to be a good father. Not the guy working 55-60 hours a week to keep food on the table for kids who weren't even his. Just another character in a murder plot that made good television.

And in a few short months, that story would explode!

When it did, it wouldn't matter that I was innocent. It wouldn't matter that I'd been manipulated and lied to. All that would matter was that I was there, in the house, with the kids, looking like I belonged.

Looking guilty.

But back then, in my townhouse, I still had hope. I still believed that maybe, just maybe, we could get through it.

That was my first mistake.

My second mistake would be thinking that truth was a defense against a system that had already decided I was guilty.

And my third mistake? Believing that being a good man would protect me from being destroyed as one.

Chapter **Five: Calm Before the Storm**

The system doesn't tell you when it's decided you're guilty. There's no letter, no phone call, no formal announcement. One day you're just a regular guy trying to raise a family, and the next day you're a target they've been watching for weeks. The only difference is knowledge—they know, and you don't.

That's the cruelest part. While you're living your life, believing in normalcy, they're already building their case against you.

Clawson, Michigan. You'd miss it if you blinked on the freeway, but for us, it was home. A sleepy, close-knit suburb nestled just north of Detroit. Block parties in the summer, basketball games at the middle school gym, the corner diner where the waitresses still remembered your coffee order. For a brief, fragile window of time, life actually felt normal.

Normal was dangerous for someone like me. Normal meant I'd stopped looking over my shoulder. Normal meant I believed I'd finally built something that couldn't be taken away.

I had planted roots without even realizing it. Jenna was doing well. The girls were adjusting. Judy was working part-time at a local office, and I was managing Applebee's just down the road. It wasn't glamorous, but it gave me purpose. A paycheck. A role in the community.

More than purpose—it gave me identity. For the first time in years, I wasn't defined by my addiction or my mistakes. I was just Greg from Applebee's, the guy who made sure your order was right and your kids got extra whipped cream on their sundaes.

People knew me. I was the friendly face behind the bar, the guy who remembered your kid's favorite milkshake or gave a free appetizer when you celebrated an anniversary. The regulars called me "Slick" because of my hair, and the younger servers looked to me as some kind of reluctant mentor. I didn't mind it.

I liked being someone people could count on. It felt like redemption after years of being the guy who let people down. Every satisfied customer, every server I trained, every shift that ran smoothly—it all felt like evidence that I was becoming the man Jenna deserved as a father.

Even the cops knew me—Detective Skagnetty, in particular. He'd been in and out of the restaurant over the years. We'd nod, exchange small talk. He coached middle school sports and showed up at all the talent shows. I even saw him at a few events where Jenna was performing. We weren't friends, not exactly—but there was a mutual respect. Or so I thought.

"How's the family?" he'd ask when he came in for his usual coffee and pie. "Jenna still singing?" Pleasant conversation that made me feel like I belonged in this community, like I was one of the good guys he didn't have to worry about.

I had no idea he was already worrying about me plenty.

That fall, I had no clue that Skagnetti was watching me more closely than I ever imagined.

While I was pouring his coffee and asking about his kids' games, he was making mental notes. Filing away details. Building a profile of Gregory Paul that would fit perfectly into the narrative they were constructing.

In the evenings, we'd do family things—walks to the park, movie nights, Sunday breakfast runs to Leo's Coney Island. Summers were spent at the local wave pool or grilling out back. I wasn't just playing house anymore. I was building a life, brick by brick, moment by moment.

Those Sunday mornings at Leo's were sacred to me. Jenna would order the same thing every time— blueberry pancakes with extra syrup. The girls would fight over who got to sit next to me in the booth. Judy would actually relax, laughing at their antics instead of looking haunted by whatever phone call she'd taken the night before.

For those few hours, we looked like what we were supposed to be—a blended family making it work against the odds.

And there was a strange comfort in the repetition. Wake up. Get the girls off to school. Clock in at Applebee's. Work 10-12 hours. Come home. Help with homework. Eat. Sleep. Repeat.

The routine was my armor against chaos. I had Tuesday and Friday off each week. As long as I could maintain the schedule, as long as everyone was where they were supposed to be when they were supposed to be there, I could pretend we were stable. Normal. Safe.

But under the surface, the cracks were spreading faster than I could patch them.

Judy had become more withdrawn. Not cold, just... distracted. She would take long phone calls outside, always pacing. She'd head out late at night, claiming she needed fresh air. More lawyers. More secrets. But I didn't ask. I had learned by then that questions led to lies, and lies led to fights. So I kept my head down. Played the part.

The late-night calls were getting more frequent. I'd watch her through the kitchen window, gesturing frantically at whoever was on the other end. Sometimes she'd be crying when she came back inside. "Everything okay?" I'd ask. "Just family stuff," she'd say, which had become her code for "don't ask because I can't tell you the truth."

I was becoming an expert at not asking the right questions.

Looking back now, I realize how many signs I missed. How many red flags I explained away because I wanted so badly to believe that we were okay.

Explained away or ignored completely. The way she jumped when the doorbell rang. The way she'd go pale when certain commercials came on—crime shows, news stories about murder cases. The way she'd suddenly change the subject when anyone mentioned Indiana.

I told myself she was still processing trauma from her past. I never considered that she might be processing guilt.

One particular night stands out. It was Jenna's school talent show. She was going to sing "Can't Stop" by the Red Hot Chili Peppers. She practiced for weeks, rehearsing in front of the living room mirror. I was so damn proud of her. RHCP is one of her favorite bands. (Thanks, Dad!) She wore a white dress with blue ribbons, and she looked like something out of a dream.

Those weeks of practice were some of the happiest I'd seen her. She'd sing while doing dishes, hum the melody while doing homework. "Dad, do you think I'm ready?" she'd ask every few days, and I'd tell her she was born ready.

Because she was—not just for the talent show, but for anything life threw at her.

She had this light in her eyes that reminded me of why I was fighting so hard to keep our family together.

As I sat in the bleachers, surrounded by other parents with their camcorders and bouquets, I saw Skagnetti across the gym. He gave me a slight nod, then turned away. Nothing unusual—except this time, he didn't smile. It was a look I hadn't seen before. Stern. Focused.

Like he was studying me instead of greeting me. Like he was seeing something I couldn't see—or maybe seeing me the way he'd been trained to see suspects instead of neighbors.

The worst part? I smiled and waved back like nothing had changed. Because to me, nothing had.

That night, I brushed it off. Maybe he'd had a long day. Maybe it was nothing.

It wasn't.

It was everything. That look was the moment I went from Greg, the friendly restaurant manager, to Greg, the person of interest. From respected community member to potential criminal. I just didn't know it yet.

In hindsight, the storm was already forming just beyond the horizon. The calm wasn't peace—it was paralysis. A waiting room before the operating table. And I was too blinded by normalcy to see the scalpel in the surgeon's hand.

What I didn't know at the time—what I couldn't have possibly known—was that my IP address had already been flagged. The Michigan State Police had already begun tracking our home internet. Federal agents were in the loop.

Judy's involvement in her husband's murder case was back on the radar. The dominoes were already falling, one by one.

They were building two cases simultaneously. Judy for conspiracy to commit murder in Indiana. And me, for something I forgot about —for something I didn't even know was a crime yet. Something that would destroy everything I'd built and separate me from my daughter forever.

While I was helping with homework and planning weekend trips to the zoo, they were planning my destruction. While I was teaching Jenna to be strong and kind and brave, they were preparing to teach her that her father was a monster.

All I knew was the sound of Jenna's laugh, the smell of pancakes on Sunday morning, the familiar chatter of the Applebee's kitchen on a Saturday night. I knew her hand in mine while walking down the sidewalk, the warm weight of the girls piled on the couch during movie night, Judy humming to herself while folding laundry.

I knew the illusion.

And God, what a beautiful illusion it was. Tiffany helping Jenna with her math homework. The younger girls begging me to push them higher on the swings. Judy actually smiling during family dinners, looking like the woman I'd fallen in love with instead of the stranger carrying all those secrets.

For those few months, I got to be the father I'd always wanted to be—not just to Jenna, but to all of them. I got to believe that love could overcome anything, that good intentions were enough, that building a family was simple as long as you cared enough to try.

And illusions are warm—right up until they shatter.

Waiting in Exile

I wasn't ready. I wasn't even close.

How do you prepare for the moment when everything you believe about your life turns out to be a lie? When the system you trusted to protect innocent people decides you're one of the guilty ones? When being a good father becomes evidence of being a predator?

You don't. You can't. You just live in the calm, believing it's peace instead of the eye of a hurricane.

The raid was coming.

But that was still a few weeks away.

For now, I let myself believe in the lie of peace.

Because when you've lived through chaos, even silence can feel like a blessing.

What I didn't understand yet was that this silence wasn't a blessing. It was a countdown. Every normal day, every family dinner, every bedtime story was one day closer to the moment when armed agents would kick down my door and destroy everything I'd built in the name of justice.

The system had already decided I was guilty. They just hadn't told me yet.

Chapter Six: The Raid

This is how they destroy an innocent man. Not with evidence. Not with witnesses. Not even with a crime. They destroy you with your own honesty, your own decency, your own willingness to tell the truth when lying would save you.

They make your virtues into weapons and turn them against everything you love.

I remember it was a cool fall evening in 2009, the kind of night that should've ended with family board games and hot chocolate—not police sirens and shattered illusions.

The date burns in my memory like a brand. October 15th, 2009. The last night I would ever be just Greg, father, and restaurant manager. Tomorrow, I would wake up as Greg, registered sex offender. Gregory Paul, the man who lost his daughter to a system that doesn't distinguish between monsters and the people who have the misfortune of living with them.

The fireplace crackled in the background as the girls cleaned up after dinner, wiping down the table and humming along to the faint music playing on the radio. I had just eased into the couch, planning to help with homework once the dishes were done. It was one of those rare nights where everything felt... settled.

Jenna was in her room working on a science project about the solar system. She'd been cutting out pictures of planets all week, carefully arranging them in order from the sun. Tiffany was helping the younger girls with their spelling. Even Judy seemed relaxed for once, folding laundry without that haunted look in her eyes.

For exactly twenty-three minutes, I got to believe we were a normal family having a normal Tuesday night.

Waiting in Exile

Then came the knock.

No, not a knock. A battering ram of fists slamming into my front door, echoing through the house like a gunshot. My stomach turned to ice.

"Police! Open up!" The voice was so loud it seemed to come from everywhere at once. The girls froze. Judy went white. Jenna was not there.

"Everyone, stay where you are!" I called back, trying to keep my voice calm even though my hands were shaking as I walked to the door.

I thought it was about Judy. Had to be. Finally, Indiana had come to collect her for her second husband's murder. Part of me was almost relieved—the lies could finally stop, the secrets could come out, and maybe we could rebuild something honest from whatever was left.

I had no idea they were there for me, too.

When I opened the door, they flooded in—a multi-state task force, Michigan State Police, Clawson detectives, and the FBI. It wasn't just a search. It was a frigging siege! They swept through the house like a SWAT team, snatching up phones, laptops, hard drives—anything with a plug or a wire. They photographed every room, questioned every person. They turned my home into a crime scene.

Nine agents. I counted them later when I was trying to make sense of what had happened. Nine law enforcement officers were here to arrest one restaurant manager who'd never been in trouble beyond a drunk driving charge fifteen years earlier.

They lined the girls up on the couch like suspects. Courtney was crying. Tiffany was too scared to make a sound. Erica kept asking, "Gre... Dad, what did we do wrong?" and I didn't have an answer because I didn't know either.

But they didn't take me away. Not yet.

"We need to talk," Detective Skagnetti said—the same man who'd been ordering coffee and cake from me for years, asking about Jenna's singing, complaining about his diet. Now he was looking at me like I was something he'd scraped off his shoe.

"Greg," he said, using my first name like we were still neighbors, "we need you to be honest with us."

Instead, they cornered me and said they'd found three video files buried on my computer.

My blood went cold.

Three files. Out of thousands and thousands of music tracks, movies, software programs, and random digital junk I'd downloaded over the years. Three files that would destroy everything I'd built, everything I'd fought for, everything I'd believed about truth, justice, and the American way.

I knew what they were referring to. Files I had stumbled across years ago—mixed in with massive download bundles on LimeWire. I never sought them out. I never shared them. I never created them. But they were there, buried like landmines in the digital pile.

LimeWire was chaotic in those days. You'd search for a song and get back a thousand results—legitimate music mixed with viruses, malware, mislabeled files, and worse. I'd downloaded entire albums, software packages, and movie collections. Most of it was junk. Some of it was corrupted. And some of it—three files out of thousands—was nightmare fuel that I'd never asked for and never wanted to see.

The smart thing would have been to lie. To deny everything. To demand lawyers, warrants, and due process. To act like the guilty men they were used to dealing with.

Instead, I did what my father had taught me to do when confronted with wrongdoing: I told the truth.

I had done what felt right—I told the truth.

"Yeah," I said. "They've been there for years. I didn't watch them again. I just let them be, and hoped this would never happen."

But it *was happening*. And it was about to get a whole lot worse.

I explained how I'd found them, how I'd been horrified, how I'd never accessed them again. I told them about the downloads, about LimeWire's random file mixing, about how I'd simply ignored them rather than seeking them out. I was honest because I thought honesty mattered. Because I thought truth was a defense.

Because I was still naïve enough to believe the system was designed to protect innocent people.

The agent didn't blink. "Good," he said. "This will be easy."

That's when I knew.

I was cooked.

"Easy." He said. Not "we'll get to the bottom of this" or "we'll investigate thoroughly." Easy. Because they didn't need to investigate. They didn't need to determine intent or context or whether I was a danger to anyone. They just needed a confession, and I'd handed it to them on a silver platter.

My honesty—the thing I'd built my recovery on, the thing I'd taught Jenna was more important than comfort—had just destroyed us both.

And as if that wasn't enough, the next words from their mouths shattered my soul.

"Do you know who Judy really is?"

I blinked. "I know her son Daniel's in jail," I said. "He killed his stepdad, right?"

They nodded—but not with understanding. With pity.

It was the pity that scared me more than the questions. Pity meant I was about to learn something that would change everything I thought I knew about my life.

"You don't know the whole story," one of them said.

Then they laid it all out. Judy wasn't just a grieving mother. She was a co-conspirator in a cold-blooded murder.

Her son Daniel had pulled the trigger. Her daughter Christina had hidden the gun. And Judy? Judy helped plan the whole thing. A calculated hit on her second husband in Merrillville, Indiana. They had tried to make it look like an accident—more than once. They wanted the money: a multi-million dollar life insurance policy and control over his Kirby vacuum sales business.

Murder for hire, essentially. Except that the killers were family members and the payment was inheritance money. Cold, calculated, and planned with the kind of detail that makes prosecutors salivate and juries vote guilty without leaving the box.

"How long have you been living with her?" Skagnetti asked.

"Two years," I said, my voice barely a whisper.

"Two years," he repeated, like he was filing it away for later use. "And you had no idea."

It wasn't a question. It was an accusation disguised as sympathy.

They covered it all up, including with me. Judy lied to my face. Lied while I cooked their dinners. Lied while I tucked her children into bed and paid their rent and tried to build a family out of the ashes of theirs.

And I treated them like gold.

They ruined my life.

Every gentle moment had been a performance. Every family dinner had been theater. Every time I'd defended Judy to my friends who thought she was "a little off," every time I'd made excuses for her strange behavior, every time I'd chosen love over suspicion—I'd been played by a master manipulator.

The woman I'd shared a bed with for two years was capable of orchestrating murder. And I'd never seen it coming.

I had no idea I was living with someone who would later appear on "Snapped" and "Mastermind of Murder." I had no clue that I was sharing a home with a woman who orchestrated her husband's death and dragged her own kids into the bloodshed.

Television shows. That's what my life had become—fodder for true crime entertainment. Judy would get her fifteen minutes of fame as the murderous mother, and I would be forever branded as the predator who lived in the same house. Guilt by association, amplified by those three damned files.

I thought I was helping a woman rebuild.

Instead, I was standing in the wreckage she created.

And now I was part of that wreckage. Not just collateral damage, but evidence. Proof that Judy's house was a place where bad things happened, where criminals lived, where children weren't safe. The narrative wrote itself: if one resident was a murderer and another was a sex offender, what kind of hellscape were those innocent kids living in?

Except I wasn't a sex offender. I was just a man who'd told the truth about three files he'd never wanted to see.

That night, as the agents combed through my things, I realized that none of this—the investigation, the raid, the charges—would have happened if I had known the truth from the beginning. If Judy had told me who she really was. If I hadn't trusted her. If I hadn't let her in.

But I had.

If I had been the kind of man who runs background checks on women he's dating. If I had been suspicious instead of hopeful. If I had been selfish instead of trying to build a family for Jenna.

If I had been anything other than exactly who I was— a recovering addict trying to be a good father—I might have avoided this trap.

But I hadn't.

And now I was being crucified for a crime I didn't commit and for files I never sought out—just because I told the truth.

Waiting in Exile

The crime I didn't commit was being a predator. The crime I did commit was being honest about three files in a sea of digital chaos. But in the eyes of the law, honesty about possession was the same as guilt about intent. Context didn't matter. Intent didn't matter. The fact that I'd never harmed a child, never sought out illegal material, never done anything but try to be a good dad to four innocent kids—none of that mattered.

All that mattered was that I'd said "yes" when they asked if the files were there.

The worst part? They didn't even care about the truth. They didn't care that Child Protective Services interviewed all the children in that home and found no evidence of abuse or misconduct on my part. They didn't care that the Clawson Police and State Police cleared me of wrongdoing. ICPS spent hours with each child. Professional interviews, psychological evaluations, and medical exams. Jenna, Tiffany, Erica, Courtney—all of them questioned by trained specialists looking for any sign that I had harmed them in any way.

The result? Nothing. No evidence of abuse, no signs of trauma, no indication whatsoever that I was anything other than what I appeared to be: a father figure who genuinely cared about their wellbeing. I was actually still *allowed* to be around Jenna and the kids. That never changed.

But evidence of innocence doesn't make headlines. It doesn't close cases. It doesn't satisfy a public hungry for monsters to blame.

They didn't care that I was the one who protected those kids.

They just wanted a name. A headline. A win. A new belt and suspenders.

And I was the easiest target on the board.

The perfect storm of circumstance and stupidity. Living with a murderer gave me proximity to crime. Telling the truth about the files gave them a confession. Being a recovering addict with a history of questioning authority made me unsympathetic. And being a man who genuinely cared about children made the charges seem especially heinous.

I was every prosecutor's dream defendant: guilty of something, honest about everything, and sympathetic to no one.

The files were there. I admitted it. Done.

Guilty.

Not guilty of seeking them out. Not guilty of viewing them again. Not guilty of sharing them, creating them, or using them to harm anyone. Just guilty of having them and being stupid enough to admit it. In the American justice system, that's all they need. Of course, I deleted them. However, they never leave your hard drive. When you download something, it is permanently etched with a digital signature, no matter what. I *should* have thrown it in the river or lit it on fire. It was a brand-new state-of-the-art Apple desktop —how was I supposed to know I'd meet the Black Widow herself??

Everything I had worked for was gone. My job. My home. My daughter. My name. My future. The only thing left was the label.

And Jenna.

Jenna, who would wake up tomorrow to find news vans in the driveway and reporters asking her classmates what it was like to live with a monster. Jenna, who would learn that her father—the man who taught her to be honest, to be kind, to believe in justice—was now the kind of person parents warn their children about.

Jenna, who was still so young. Who had no idea what was happening. Who would eventually hear the twisted version of the story, passed through a hundred mouths and a thousand rumors, until it sounded like I was the monster they wanted me to be.

How do you explain to a ten-year-old that her father isn't a predator, he's just a man who made the mistake of being honest with people who weaponize honesty? How do you tell her that the system she's been taught to trust and respect has just destroyed her family for no reason other than convenience?

You don't. You can't. You just disappear from her life and hope that someday, when she's older, she'll understand that loving her was the only thing I ever did right.

The real monsters? They got their fifteen minutes on cable TV. Judy was sentenced to decades in prison. The oldest daughter, Christina, took her own life. Daniel did his time for pulling the trigger, then faded into obscurity. Tiffany got emancipated at 16. Erica went to Florida to live with Grandpa. And, Courtney, was a live-in family friend who had to go back to her family's dysfunction. What a mess!

Judy became a cautionary tale about greed and family dysfunction. Daniel and Christina became examples of what happens when children are corrupted by adult evil. They were pitied, studied, and analyzed by criminal psychologists and true crime enthusiasts.

Their story had a moral: money corrupts, murder destroys families, justice eventually prevails.

My story had a different moral: honesty is dangerous, good intentions don't matter, and sometimes justice is just revenge wearing a badge, seeking accolades & recognition.

And me? I was left to rot on the sex offender registry. Left to carry the weight of her lies. Left to endure the permanent exile from my own child's life.

The registry. Twenty-five years of checking in with law enforcement, having my address published online, being banned from parks and schools, and anywhere children might be present. Twenty-five years of being unemployable, unrentable, unforgettable. Twenty-five years of wearing a scarlet letter for a crime I didn't commit, punishment for files I never sought.

Twenty-five years of exile from Jenna's life.

They didn't just knock on my door that night.

They erased me.

And they called it justice.

Justice. The word tastes like ashes in my mouth now. Justice would have been investigating before raiding. Justice would have been distinguishing between accidentally possessing something and intentionally seeking it out. Justice would have been protecting the innocent while punishing the guilty.

What they gave me wasn't justice. It was efficiency. It was convenient. It was the system working exactly as designed—not to find truth, but to process cases and satisfy statistics and give the public someone to blame.

I call it betrayal.

Waiting in Exile

I call it exile.

I call it the night the truth stopped mattering.

I call it the night America failed a father who was trying to do right by four innocent children.

And I call it the beginning of twenty-five years in the wilderness, wondering if Jenna will ever forgive me for telling the truth.

Chapter Seven: The Fallout

This is how they finish destroying you. The raid was just the beginning—the shock and awe. The real destruction comes after, slow and methodical, like a cancer eating through everything you've built. They don't need to convict you to ruin you. The accusation is enough.

The system knows this. They count on it.

After the raid, the walls didn't just close in—they collapsed. The air inside that house never felt breathable again. Every floorboard creaked with suspicion, every shadow whispered shame. I wasn't arrested that night, but I might as well have been. My freedom became a waiting room for judgment, and my life—a cautionary tale no one wanted to hear.

The house felt contaminated. Not by what I'd done—I hadn't done anything—but by what they'd accused me of. It was like they'd left radioactive dust on everything they'd touched. The couch where we'd watched movies together. The kitchen table where I'd helped with homework. Jenna's bedroom door, which I now avoided walking past because it felt wrong, dangerous, like proximity to innocence was evidence of guilt. The entire house was ransacked.

For days, I walked around in a daze, replaying every moment of the raid, every word the agents said, every corner of my house they tore apart. I felt like a ghost in my own home. Judy's kids, still unaware of the full gravity of what their mother had done, kept trying to carry on like things were normal—watching TV, doing homework, asking what was for dinner. But I couldn't eat. I couldn't sleep. My mind was unraveling.

Waiting in Exile

"Dad Greg, are you okay?" Tiffany asked me one morning, finding me staring at my untouched coffee. She was thirteen, old enough to sense that something fundamental had shifted, but too young to understand what.

"I'm fine, sweetheart," I lied, because what else could I say? How do you explain to a child that the man who's been her father figure for two years is now considered too dangerous to be around children?

But I wasn't fine. I was disappearing. Each day, a little more of who I'd been vanished, replaced by this hollow thing that jumped at every knock on the door, every phone call, every car that slowed down in front of the house.

And then, almost on cue, the world started to follow.

The news broke on a Thursday. Local news first—"Multi-State Task Force Raids Clawson Home"—then the details started leaking. My name. My address. The charges that hadn't even been filed yet. By Friday, my neighbors knew. By Monday, my coworkers knew. By the end of the week, everyone in Clawson knew.

Gregory Paul. The guy from Applebee's. The one with the nice daughter who sang at the talent shows. Sex offender. Upper management quickly found reasons why I should be fired. One write-up after another. Instead of approaching me as a man—the man they came to depend upon, the funny guy with a heart of gold—instead of innocence before guilt, they treated me as a dangerous reptile. A huge pest to be disposed of.

Word spreads fast in a town like Clawson. Faster than truth. The small-town grapevine became a noose around my neck. I walked into Applebee's for my shift and could feel the tension. Whispers behind menus. Coworkers who suddenly wouldn't meet my eye. It didn't take long before I was pulled into the office by my GM's boss, Tanner. He looked uncomfortable, but firm.

Tanner had hired me five years earlier. We'd worked together through busy Saturday nights and crazy holiday rushes. He'd trusted me with cash deposits and key holder responsibilities. He'd even asked my advice about his own relationship problems. Now he couldn't look me in the eye.

"We've received a complaint," he said.

"A complaint?"

"An accusation. Sexual harassment."

My heart dropped.

Sexual harassment. Not the child pornography charges—they couldn't fire me for accusations that hadn't been proven in court. But sexual harassment? That was immediate grounds for termination. Clean and simple. No due process required.

"From who?"

"I can't tell you that."

"Of course you can't."

Of course, they couldn't. Because there probably wasn't a "who." There was just a company that needed to distance itself from a liability, and sexual harassment was the easiest way to make it happen. Anonymous complaints are impossible to defend against.

I knew what this was. It wasn't about harassment. It was about what the cops found. Or thought they found. Or wanted people to believe they found. It was the stain they left behind—on my name, on my reputation, on my life. I was radioactive.

Radioactive. That's exactly what it felt like. Like I was emitting something dangerous that contaminated everyone who came too close. My servers suddenly had reasons to avoid the shifts I was managing. Customers complained about things that had never been problems before. The whole restaurant ecosystem was rejecting me like a bad organ.

Weeks passed. The pressure built. Then came the second meeting with Tanner. This time, he had a list. Things I supposedly did wrong on the job—late clock-ins, poor performance, failure to follow company policy.

The list was impressive in its creativity. Late by three minutes on a Tuesday two months ago. Failed to follow up on a customer complaint that I'd never been told about. Poor attitude during staff meetings where I'd apparently been "sullen and unresponsive," which was management-speak for "looked tired after being raided by the FBI."

They'd been building a paper trail, carefully documenting every minor infraction, every moment of human imperfection, so they could fire me for cause instead of admitting they were firing me for being accused of a crime.

I was fired.

And just like that, my livelihood vanished.

Twenty-three years in restaurant management. Spotless record until the moment I became a liability. All of it was gone because someone decided I was guilty before I'd even been charged.

I filed for unemployment, and they fought me on that, too. They took it to mediation. I stood in front of the board and laid out my case—my spotless record, my years of service, the lies they were using to ruin me. And somehow, I won. I won my unemployment. But I was still broke. Still broken. Still branded.

Winning the unemployment hearing felt like a small miracle—the first time in weeks that someone in an official capacity had listened to me and decided I was telling the truth. The hearing officer actually looked angry when she heard about the "anonymous sexual harassment complaint" that conveniently appeared after the raid.

"Mr. Paul," she said, "it appears to me that this employer is manufacturing reasons to terminate you. You'll receive your benefits."

It was a tiny victory in an ocean of defeats. But it was something.

Not long after that, I managed to land a job at the Olive Garden in Novi. I was hired as the front-of-house manager. It felt like a fresh start—briefly. I made a few friends. Built a little rhythm. Smiled a little more.

The interview went well. The GM, Mike, seemed impressed by my experience. He didn't ask about why I'd left Applebee's, and I didn't volunteer the information. For three weeks, I actually felt human again. I had purpose, a paycheck, and coworkers who treated me like a normal person instead of a walking disease.

I should have known it wouldn't last.

But then, it happened again.

Someone found out. The whispers began. The glances. The sideways smirks. Then came the phone calls—nasty, anonymous ones. And the car keying. The lawn sign that showed up one day outside the house.

It read: "SEX OFFENDER LIVES HERE."

Waiting in Exile

The sign appeared on a Tuesday morning. Professionally made, like they'd ordered it online. Planted in the front yard with the precision of a campaign advertisement. The neighbors saw it before I did. By the time I got home from work, three people had already called to "check on me" with voices full of fake concern and genuine excitement.

Someone had done their research. Found out where Gregory Paul lived and decided to be the neighborhood vigilante. The sign wasn't just about me—it was about anyone who might be harboring a monster. It was terrorism, pure and simple.

I left the job before they could fire me.

Mike called me into her office on a Friday afternoon. "Greg," he said, looking uncomfortable, "we need to talk." I could see the termination paperwork already printed on his desk.

"Don't," I said. "I'll make this easy for everyone." I took off my name tag and walked out.

It was easier than being fired again. Easier than sitting through another performance about anonymous complaints and company policies. I had whatever dignity was left to preserve.

After that, I stopped trying. I panhandled a few times just to eat. Pride had long since left the building. Dignity was a luxury I couldn't afford.

Panhandling. Me. The guy who used to lecture Jenna about working hard and being responsible. Standing outside gas stations with a cardboard sign, hoping strangers would spare some change. The looks of disgust from people who recognized me were almost worse than the hunger.

But hunger is hunger. And when you're unemployable, unemployed, and running out of savings, pride becomes irrelevant pretty quickly.

Meanwhile, Judy's world was unraveling too. The FBI finally gave her an ultimatum—turn herself in or they'd come get her. She chose to surrender. I drove her and the kids to the Indiana Women's Prison. Watching her walk in was surreal. I couldn't believe I had once thought she was the love of my life. Now she was just another headline.

That drive to Indiana was the longest four hours of my life. The kids were crying in the backseat. Judy was silent, staring out the window like she was already gone. And I was driving the woman who'd destroyed my life to her final destination, because somehow I was still the only responsible adult left in their world.

"Take care of them," she said as we pulled into the prison parking lot.

"I can't," I told her. "They won't let me."

She nodded like she understood, but I don't think she did. I don't think she ever understood how completely she had poisoned everything she'd touched, including me.

Then came my charges.

Three counts of possession of child-abusive material. One count of using a computer to commit a felony. One count of distributing. One count of manufacturing. I was stunned. Sick. Numb.

Six felony counts. For three files I'd never sought out, never viewed after the initial accidental discovery, never shared with anyone. But the system doesn't distinguish between accidental possession and intentional collection. In their eyes, having it was the same as wanting it, wanting it was the same as using it, and using it was the same as sharing it and creating it.

The manufacturing charge was the cruelest joke of all. Apparently, when LimeWire downloaded files to my computer, the system classified that as "manufacturing" because the computer was creating new copies. Technical nonsense that turned every person who'd ever used peer-to-peer file sharing into a potential manufacturer of whatever garbage ended up in their download folder.

I paid $30,000 to a lawyer, thinking he could make it all go away. He got the distribution and manufacturing charges dropped, but said he couldn't do anything about the rest. "Take the plea," he said. "It's your best shot."

Thirty thousand dollars. Jenna's college fund, gone. My retirement savings, gone. Everything I'd saved working double shifts and managing restaurants for twenty years was handed over to a lawyer who told me from day one that I was probably going to prison no matter what.

"The system doesn't like to lose," he explained. "They've got you on possession. That's enough. We can fight it, but you'll spend more money and probably get a worse outcome. Take the plea, do your time, and try to rebuild."

Rebuild. Like starting over after a divorce, except your ex-wife was the American justice system, and the settlement included a lifetime ban from being near children.

I didn't even get to hear my sentence before the cuffs went on. They took me away right then and there in court.

The bailiff was gentle about it, at least. "Sorry, Greg," he said quietly as he fastened the handcuffs. "Just doing my job." I'd known him for years—he'd eaten at Applebee's, asked about Jenna, and complained about his back problems. Now he was arresting me.

Before they did, friends and family stood up to speak. One by one, they told the judge who I really was. A good man. A devoted father. A protector. A provider. Their words were beautiful. Heart-wrenching. But it didn't matter.

My sister Sherry cried as she talked about how I'd helped raise her daughter, Kylie. My old manager from Red Lobster testified about my character, my work ethic, and my reputation in the community. Even some of my regular customers from Applebee's showed up to speak on my behalf.

"Your Honor," Sherry said through tears, "my brother is many things, but he is not a predator. He's the man who taught my daughter to ride a bike. He's the man who worked three jobs to support Jenna. He's the man who took in a woman and her children because he believed in second chances. Don't let one mistake destroy a good man's life."

The judge listened politely, nodded appropriately, and sentenced me anyway.

I got one year in the county jail. And five years' probation. If I slipped up once, I could be facing much more.

One year. Three hundred and sixty-five days for three files I'd never wanted to see. Compare that to Judy's sentence for actually planning and executing a murder—she got thirty years, but she'd be eligible for parole in fifteen. Somehow, accidentally possessing illegal files was being punished almost as harshly as orchestrating someone's death.

The math of justice doesn't add up when you're the one being counted.

I wasn't just sentenced. I was exiled.

Waiting in Exile

Exiled from Jenna's life. Exiled from normal employment. Exiled from parks, schools, and anywhere children might be present. Exiled from the person I'd been and any hope of becoming someone better.

And the worst was yet to come.

Because jail was just the appetizer. The real punishment—the registry, the permanent status as a registered sex offender, the lifetime of suspicion and restriction—that was the main course. And it would never end.

Twenty-four years and counting.

Gregory Paul

Chapter Eight: Cage Life

This is what happens when the system has finally caught you. After the raid, after the accusations, after the character assassination and the manufactured firing and the community vigilantism—this is where they put you. Not to rehabilitate you. Not to make you better. Just to warehouse you with the discarded and the forgotten until your time is up.

And if you're lucky, you survive it with something resembling a soul still intact.

Jail isn't what you see on television. It's not orange jumpsuits and cafeteria brawls with a background score. It's colder. Cruder. More humiliating. More dehumanizing than any script could do justice. From the moment they walked me into that jail, shackled and processed, I ceased to be a person. I became a number. A cautionary tale. A piece of meat in a 10-man cage crammed with 15.

Inmate 2009-4457. That's who I was now. Not Gregory, not Dad, not the guy who used to manage restaurants and remember your kid's favorite milkshake. Just another file number in a system designed to strip away everything that made you human.

The intake process alone was designed to break you down. Strip search. Cavity search. Delousing shower with industrial soap that burns your skin. Jumpsuit that didn't fit. Bedding that smelled like industrial bleach and other people's misery. By the time they threw me in the cell, I felt like I'd been disassembled and put back together like a used pinball machine.

There was no room to breathe, let alone move. Five of us slept on the floor in "boats"—those plastic, canoe-shaped boxes that barely fit a grown man. They handed me one itchy blanket, one sheet, and a pillow so thin it could've been a napkin. Sleep didn't come easy. Not with the constant noise, the bickering, the scraping of plastic against concrete. Fights broke out almost every day. Some loud and flashy. Others, cold and calculated. The kind of violence that brews from boredom and broken spirits.

The boats were the worst part. Imagine trying to sleep in a bathtub that's too small, surrounded by fourteen other men who haven't showered in days, while fluorescent lights buzz overhead eighteen hours a day. The smell was indescribable—sweat, fear, anger, institutional disinfectant, and something else I couldn't identify but suspected was despair.

My bunkmate was a kid named Tommy who'd been caught dealing meth to pay for his daughter's medical bills. His wife had divorced him while he was inside. He cried himself to sleep every night for the first two weeks, then went silent for the next month. I watched him disappear a little more each day, until he was just another ghost shuffling through the motions.

They kept us locked down for 23 hours a day. One hour of "rec," if you could call it that. Most days they skipped it altogether, tossing us out two at a time just to walk in circles. Hands shackled around a waist chain. Ankle cuffs to finish the ensemble. I had never felt more humiliated in my life. Even the air seemed to mock me.

Rec time was a joke. A concrete box with a basketball hoop but no ball, chain-link ceiling so you couldn't see the sky properly, guards watching from towers like you were an animal in a zoo. Some days they'd "forget" to let us out. Some days they'd cut it short because of "security concerns."

Most days you were so desperate for fresh air that even twenty minutes of walking in shackles felt like freedom.

The worst part was knowing that somewhere outside those walls, Jenna was going to school, doing homework, maybe wondering why her dad had disappeared from her life. While I was walking in circles like a trained seal, she was growing up without me.

One day, they brought in a new guy. A monster. About 5'11", 250 pounds of solid, angry muscle. The kind of guy who does 50 push-ups before breakfast just to calm down. He came in swinging—literally. Punching the air, yelling at the walls, looking for a fight like it was his morning coffee. He scared the hell out of everyone.

His name was Marcus, though nobody dared use it. He'd been in and out of county jails since he was eighteen, knew the system, knew how to work it. Prison tattoos covered his arms and neck—not the artistic kind you see on TV, but crude, jailhouse ink that looked like scars. He walked like he owned every inch of space he occupied, and maybe he did.

"Fresh meat," he announced when he saw me reading in my bunk. "What you in for, dawg-nuts?"

I didn't answer. I'd learned that silence was sometimes the safest response. But silence can be interpreted as weakness, and weakness was dangerous.

He beat up two guys in one day for no reason. Just a glare, or a misstep near his bunk. I watched it all from the corner, minding my own, staying alert. But you can't stay invisible forever.

The first guy was Tommy, my bunkmate. Marcus decided Tommy was looking at him wrong during dinner. Broke his nose with a headbutt so fast the guards didn't even see it coming. Tommy spent three days in the infirmary and came back even quieter than before.

The second was an older guy named Pete who made the mistake of sitting in "Marcus's" spot during the evening news. Marcus picked him up and threw him into the concrete wall like he weighed nothing. Pete spent a week in medical. When he came back, he couldn't use his left arm properly.

I knew I was next. It was just a matter of when.

When he came at me, it wasn't screaming or charging. It was little jabs. Insults. Provocations. I tried to hold my tongue. I did. But he kept pushing. And when he finally shoved me, that switch flipped.

"You scared of me, old man?" he whispered during mail call, standing too close, breathing down my neck. "You look scared."

"I'm not scared of you," I said quietly.

"No? Then why you shaking?"

I wasn't shaking. But I could feel the energy building, that familiar pre-fight tension that starts in your stomach and spreads through your whole body. I'd felt it before, in bars and parking lots back in my drinking days. The moment when talking stops working and something primitive takes over.

"Maybe you need to learn some respect," he said, and gave me a hard shove that sent me stumbling into the wall.

That's when the switch flipped.

We tangled. It started as a wrestling match, but it escalated quickly into raw, primal chaos. Fists flew. I was nearly out of breath, overwhelmed by his size and power. But I had already rehearsed this fight in my mind the day

Gregory Paul

Tommy came back. I had my training. I knew technique. So I dropped to the floor, locked my legs over his neck and torso, and yanked his arm with every ounce of rage I'd stored since the day of the raid. I locked in a textbook armbar, the kind you see in MMA bouts. And he tapped. Oh, he tapped.

The fight lasted maybe ninety seconds, but it felt like an hour. Marcus had fifty pounds on me, but he was a brawler, not a fighter. All muscle, no technique. When I dropped for the armbar, he followed me down like I knew he would, putting all his weight into trying to ground and pound me.

Big mistake.

I wrapped my legs around his neck and grabbed his arm with both hands, hyperextending the elbow joint until I felt something give. Not break—just give. Enough to let him know I could break it if I wanted to.

"Tap out or I snap it," I said through gritted teeth.

He tapped. Fast. Frantically. Like his life depended on it.

The others pulled me off him. His face was a mess. Bleeding. Purple. Eyes swollen shut. And for the first time in weeks months, I felt... seen. Like maybe I wasn't just some forgotten ghost in a cage. I was still me. Still someone.

Still dangerous when I needed to be.

"Jesus Christ," someone whispered. "Where'd you learn to fight like that?"

I didn't answer. But for the first time since the raid, I felt like Gregory Paul instead of Inmate 2009-4457. For ninety seconds, I'd been something other than a victim.

But it was far from over.

Marcus spent two days in the infirmary. When he came back, his arm in a sling, he walked straight up to my bunk.

Waiting in Exile

"Respect," he said, and nodded once. After that, he left me alone. More than alone—he made sure everyone else left me alone too. Prison politics are strange and brutal, but sometimes they work in your favor.

I'd earned something that couldn't be taken away: the knowledge that I could still fight for myself when it mattered.

That year in jail was the worst time of my life. Worse than the trial. Worse than the raid. Worse than the heartbreak that came after. Because in there, I broke. Mentally. Emotionally. Spiritually. I had a full-blown breakdown. I stopped eating. I stopped talking. I stopped caring. I became a shadow.

The breakdown came about three months in. One morning I woke up and couldn't remember why I was trying to survive. Couldn't remember what I was fighting for. Jenna felt like a dream from someone else's life. The restaurant, the house in Clawson, the man I'd been—all of it felt like a movie I'd watched once, a long time ago.

I stopped showering. Stopped leaving my bunk except to use the bathroom. Stopped responding when people talked to me. The guards noticed, but they didn't care. Depression wasn't their problem. They had quotas to meet and shifts to survive.

I was disappearing, one day at a time.

But I clung to something—my daughter, Jenna.

Jenna was my lifeline, even though she felt impossibly far away. Some nights I'd lie awake and try to remember her voice, the way she laughed, the sound she made when she was concentrating on homework. I'd close my eyes and try to smell her shampoo, that beautiful scent that used to cling to my shirts after I hugged her goodnight.

Gregory Paul

I had to believe she was still out there, still real, still mine.

I started writing her letters. Every day. I wouldn't send them daily, but I poured my soul into them and mailed a week's worth at a time. I needed her to know I was still alive. That I hadn't given up. That somewhere, beneath the accusations and the label, her dad was still there.

"Dear Jenna," every letter began. "Today I woke up and the first thing I thought about was you."

I wrote about everything and nothing. What I ate for breakfast (if I ate). What I was reading. What I missed about the outside world. What I remembered about our time together. I wrote about the tent in her bedroom, about her singing "Red Hot Chili Peppers," about Sunday mornings at Leo's Coney Island.

I wrote about how sorry I was. How none of this was her fault. How proud I was of her, even though I wasn't there to see her growing up.

Most importantly, I wrote about hope. That someday, when all this was over, we'd find our way back to each other.

I read books too. Nine of them. 20,000 Leagues Under the Sea, Moby Dick, Lord of the Flies, The Bible. I turned my jail time into a prison classroom of purpose. I started doing book reports, hoping Jenna might read the same stories and feel closer to me. That we could build some imaginary bridge between cells and suburbs, between my cage and her life.

The jail library was a joke—maybe fifty books total, most of them falling apart, half the pages missing from anything remotely interesting. But I read everything they had. Fiction, non-fiction, outdated legal texts, even romance novels someone had donated. Reading kept my mind active when everything else was designed to shut it down.

Waiting in Exile

Lord of the Flies hit me hardest. A story about civilization breaking down, about good people becoming savages when the rules disappear. I saw myself in Ralph, trying to maintain order and decency while everything fell apart around him. I saw the jail on the island—a place where the strong preyed on the weak and survival trumped morality.

But I also saw hope in the ending. Ralph survives. Broken, traumatized, but alive. Still human despite everything he's endured.

I hit the law library next. Studied my case. Compared it to others. Tried to understand the system that had swallowed me. What I found only added fuel to my rage. So many inconsistencies. So many people like me—railroaded, ignored, discarded.

The law library had three shelves of outdated legal books and a computer that worked maybe half the time. But I spent hours there, reading case law, studying precedents, trying to understand how three accidental files had destroyed my entire life.

What I found was a system designed for efficiency, not justice. Plea bargains that coerced innocent people into admitting guilt because fighting meant risking decades in prison. Mandatory minimums that treated every case the same regardless of context. Technical definitions that turned accidents into felonies.

I read about men who'd served twenty years for possession charges, fathers separated from their children permanently for mistakes that hurt no one. I read about actual predators who'd received lighter sentences because they had better lawyers or more sympathetic circumstances.

The system wasn't broken. It was working exactly as designed—to process people quickly and keep the public satisfied that someone was being punished, regardless of whether that someone was actually guilty of being dangerous.

I fantasized about running away. Not from jail, but from life. I dreamed of Alaska. Living off the grid. Hunting. Fishing. Surviving on my own terms. Maybe taking Jenna with me, raising her where no one could whisper my name with disgust.

Alaska became my escape. In my mind, I built a cabin by a lake, far from registries and probation officers and neighbors who looked at me like I was a disease. I'd teach Jenna to fish, to hunt, to survive in the wilderness. We'd live simply, honestly, without the weight of accusations and labels.

It was a fantasy, but it kept me sane. Gave me something to hope for beyond just surviving each day.

But I didn't realize back then that probation would be its own kind of cage. That the freedom they were offering was just exile with an ankle monitor.

Freedom. What a joke that word would become. I was already learning that there were worse things than being locked up. At least in jail, everyone was equally trapped. On the outside, I'd be the only one wearing invisible chains.

Still, I endured.

Because I had to.

Because Jenna deserved a father who didn't give up, even when giving up would have been easier.

Because somewhere in that concrete box, surrounded by broken men and broken dreams, I remembered who I was before the system got hold of me. Not perfect, not innocent of poor judgment, but not a monster either. Just a man who'd tried to build a family and made the mistake of being honest when honesty was dangerous.

And somewhere in that madness, I remembered something: I wasn't just suffering—I was being forged. Like steel in fire. Like truth in silence. Like a father who refused to vanish.

Even if the world never saw it.

Even if my daughter never read those letters.

Even if I never got another chance.

I kept going.

Because sometimes, that's all a man can do. Literally.

Gregory Paul

Chapter Nine: The Second Sentence

The greatest trick the system ever pulled was convincing the public that justice ends with sentencing. That once you've "done your time," you're free to rebuild your life. But for people like me—people labeled as sex offenders—the real punishment begins when the cell door opens.

The real sentence is life without parole.

They let me out, but they didn't set me free.

When that jail cell door finally clanged open after a year of caged existence, it didn't feel like release. It felt like a transfer. From one form of punishment to another. From orange jumpsuits and iron bars to invisible shackles and psychological warfare. Probation.

I walked out wearing the same clothes I'd worn to sentencing a year earlier. They hung loose now—I'd lost twenty pounds in jail, most of it muscle, some of it hope. The sunlight hurt my eyes. The sounds of traffic seemed impossibly loud. Everything moved too fast, like the world had sped up while I was frozen in concrete time.

I was free, technically. But freedom is relative when you're wearing an ankle monitor and everyone you meet treats you like a walking disease.

They called it "community supervision." I called it surveillance. They said it was to help me transition back into society. But society had already decided it wanted no part of me.

Community supervision. Like I was being supervised by a community that gave a damn about my success instead of being monitored by a system that counted on my failure.

Waiting in Exile

The name was just another lie in a long line of lies they told to make the process sound humane.

The first sign came early: I was ordered to undergo a psychological evaluation. Not once. Not twice. Three times. The first was with an older Indian psychiatrist—balding, glasses. He asked me to take the WAIS IQ test. I didn't even know what that was, but I took it seriously.

I scored a 126.

He raised an eyebrow. "How did you get that score?"

"Uh... I just answered the questions," I said. What else could I say? He didn't seem satisfied. He asked me to take it again.

Like intelligence was suspicious. Like scoring above average was somehow evidence of deception. In his world, sex offenders were supposed to be drooling idiots or manipulative masterminds. Normal intelligence didn't fit the profile.

The second time, I was annoyed. Rushed through the math. Got a 119.

He smiled like he had discovered something, but wouldn't say what. I told him I wanted to take it one more time—untimed. He agreed. I scored a 136. That was the last time he looked me in the eye without suspicion.

A 136 IQ puts you in the top 2% of the population. Superior intelligence, by their standards. And in the world of sex offender treatment, superior intelligence equals superior danger. Smart enough to plan, smart enough to manipulate, smart enough to hide in plain sight.

The doctor made notes after that third test. Lots of notes. I couldn't see what he was writing, but I could see his expression change. I'd gone from being a patient to being a puzzle—and not the kind anyone wanted to solve.

From that point on, I was convinced they thought I was some sort of evil genius. Not because of what I'd done—because I hadn't done anything—but because I was too normal, too articulate, too intelligent. That made me dangerous in their eyes. Not a pervert. Not a predator. Something worse.

An enigma.

The worst kind of sex offender, in their minds, was the one who didn't fit the stereotype. The one who could carry on a normal conversation, hold down a job, raise a daughter. Because if someone like me could be a predator, then anyone could be. And that was too scary a thought for most people to handle.

So they decided I must be a special kind of dangerous—the kind that hides in plain sight, that manipulates through charm and intelligence. A wolf in sheep's clothing, instead of just a sheep that had been labeled a wolf.

That's when the real torture began.

Standard protocol, they said, for sex offenders. But I wasn't like the others. I knew it. They knew it. Still, they treated me the same. Group therapy with convicted rapists. Daily logs of my thoughts. Random polygraphs. Breathalyzer tests. Drug screens.

Group therapy was the worst. Sitting in a circle with men who had actually committed horrible crimes, pretending we were all the same. The facilitator would talk about "cognitive distortions" and "victim empathy" while I sat there thinking about Jenna and wondering how many years it would be before I could take her to a park again.

"Gregory," the facilitator would say, "what cognitive distortions led to your offense?"

What cognitive distortions? The distortion that downloading music on LimeWire was legal? The distortion that telling the truth to police was the right thing to do? The distortion that the justice system actually cared about justice?

Still, they slapped an ankle monitor on me and put a breathalyzer on my table. It would beep every 30–60 minutes, demanding a clean blow. It didn't matter if Jenna was visiting. It didn't matter if we were eating dinner. Beep. Blow. Beep. Blow. It was degrading. Dehumanizing. And worst of all—it was a constant reminder to my daughter that I wasn't like the other dads.

She didn't say it at first. But eventually, she told her mother she didn't want to come over anymore.

That broke me. Again.

"It's weird there, Mom," I heard her say on the phone one day. I wasn't supposed to be listening, but sound carries in small apartments. "All those beeping things. And Dad seems... different."

Different. That's what I'd become to my own daughter. Not dangerous, not scary—just different. Strange. Other. Not the father she remembered from before the raid, but this new version who lived under electronic surveillance and couldn't take her to McDonald's without his ankle monitor going off.

It wasn't just rejection. It was confirmation. That the damage was permanent. That the system had stolen something sacred from both of us. That no matter how many times I said I was innocent, or proved I wasn't a danger, or showed up with love and intention—none of it mattered.

Because the label stuck.

Because the machine doesn't care about nuance. It only cares about compliance.

The machine had done its job perfectly. It had taken a father and daughter who loved each other and taught them to fear that love. It had made normal family time feel dangerous and wrong. It had convinced a child that her father was someone to be avoided, not because he'd hurt her, but because being near him felt uncomfortable.

That's the real genius of the registry system. It doesn't just punish the labeled—it trains everyone around them to participate in the punishment.

Then came Halloween night.

I had been on probation for about two months. Still trying to toe the line, still struggling with the humiliation, still grieving the loss of my daughter's presence in my life. I wasn't drinking. I wasn't partying. But I did have three beers in my fridge—leftover from my buddy's visit—and one Hustler DVD in my bottom drawer. A dumb relic from a dumber time.

That was all it took.

Halloween night. Kids out trick-or-treating, families enjoying normal holiday traditions, and I was sitting in my apartment trying to figure out how to rebuild a life that felt more broken every day. I'd turned off all my lights so no kids would come to my door—registered sex offenders aren't supposed to participate in children's holidays, even passively.

That's when they came.

A troop of cops, along with my probation officer, barged into my house. No warrant. No warning. They tossed the place like I was Pablo Escobar. Flipped drawers, ripped open laundry bins, kicked over furniture. They found the beers. They found the DVD.

And that was it. Violation.

"Consumption of alcohol is prohibited," my probation officer said, holding up one of the unopened beer cans like it was evidence of murder. "Possession of pornographic material is prohibited."

"I wasn't drinking," I said. "Those are left over from—"

"Doesn't matter. You're not allowed to possess alcohol. Period."

The DVD was ten years old, buried under paperwork I'd forgotten existed. Legal adult pornography that any other man in America could own without consequence. But I wasn't any other man. I was a registered sex offender, which meant normal human sexuality was now criminal.

Back to jail.

This time it was "only" 30 days. But to me, it might as well have been a year. Now they put me in general population with men who'd committed real crimes—armed robbery, assault, drug dealing. Ironically, I felt safer there than I had in the treatment programs with other "sex offenders."

After the 10-man cage, it felt like daycare. It almost felt normal. No shackles during rec. We played basketball. We played chess. I rediscovered that I was damn good at chess. Won every game. That, too, made people suspicious.

Chess became my escape. The logic of it, the pure strategy divorced from emotion or politics or social stigma. On the chessboard, intelligence was an advantage instead of evidence of hidden depravity. I could think five moves ahead without someone interpreting that as manipulation.

We made jailhouse hooch with apples, oranges, bread for yeast. It tasted like death and smelled worse. But it numbed the pain. Some guys smuggled in heroin and tobacco. That wasn't my scene. I stuck to the chessboard and the toilet wine.

The hooch was dangerous—not just because it was against the rules, but because getting caught would mean more time, more violations, more distance from Jenna. But some nights, the psychological pain was so intense that physical numbness felt like mercy.

Still, my mind wandered. Always back to Jenna. Always to the fear that she would forget me. That every passing day, I became more of a story than a person.

I'd close my eyes and try to remember her laugh, but it was getting harder. The sound was fading, replaced by the memory of her uncomfortable silence during those last few visits. I was losing her in real time, and there was nothing I could do to stop it.

That's when I realized I needed a plan.

Because probation wasn't freedom—it was a slow-motion re-incarceration.

Because therapy wasn't healing—it was control.

Because being honest hadn't saved me—it had sunk me.

Because the system wasn't designed to help me succeed—it was designed to ensure I failed, creating more violations, more time, more justification for its own existence.

So I started keeping my head down. I complied. I played the game.

Waiting in Exile

But deep down, I made a vow.

If they were going to treat me like a monster, I'd at least show them a man who survived the system. A man who walked through hell and came out holding the receipts.

A man who would never stop fighting to get back to his daughter, no matter how many times they knocked him down.

The second sentence had begun.

But it wouldn't break me.

Because somewhere out there, Jenna was growing up. And someday—somehow—I was going to find my way back to being her father.

Chapter Ten: The Lie Detector

The polygraph doesn't detect lies. It detects stress. And when you're strapped to a machine designed to prove you're a monster, when the people asking questions have already decided you're guilty, when the entire system profits from your failure—everyone's stressed. Including the innocent.

Especially the innocent.

The lie wasn't mine. But I was the one being punished for it.

By the time my second round of probation started—after that ridiculous Halloween violation—I was already a shell of who I used to be. Each time I tried to stand up straight, something yanked the chain tighter. But I kept showing up. I kept doing what they asked. I kept breathing.

What choice did I have?

By now I'd learned the rhythm of surveillance. The random visits, the drug tests, the therapy sessions where I sat next to actual predators and pretended we belonged in the same category. Every interaction was designed to catch me in some violation, some slip-up, some evidence that I was exactly what they'd labeled me.

The worst part wasn't the restrictions—it was the constant performance. Having to act grateful for their "supervision," having to pretend their treatment was helping, having to nod along when they explained how my "offense" fit their models of criminal behavior.

They brought me in again. Polygraph. "Routine," they said. It always was. But what it really meant was: We think you're hiding something, and this is how we squeeze it out of you.

Waiting in Exile

Dr. Martinez's office, third floor of the county building. The same place where they'd administered my psychological evaluations, where they'd first decided my intelligence made me dangerous. The polygraph was supposed to be scientific, objective, but it felt more like medieval torture updated for the digital age.

I sat in the chair, wires coiled around my chest and fingers like a snake getting comfortable. The room was cold. Deliberately uncomfortable. The examiner, some guy who looked like he'd rather be torturing people in Guantanamo, gave me the standard speech.

His name was Stevens, according to his badge. Thick neck, dead eyes, the kind of man who enjoyed having power over people who couldn't fight back. He'd probably been doing this for twenty years, watching stressed men sweat through interrogations, counting inconclusive results as victories.

"Just answer truthfully and you'll be fine."

I nodded. But I wasn't fine. Not because I had something to hide. But because I had nothing left to give. I was tired. Already exhausted from pretending that this was normal. That I deserved this.

"We're going to start with some baseline questions," Stevens said, adjusting the sensors. "What's your name? Where do you live? Are you sitting in a chair?"

Even the baseline questions felt like traps. Yes, I was Gregory Paul. Yes, I lived at the address they'd assigned me. Yes, I was sitting in a chair that felt like an electric chair waiting for the switch to be thrown.

The questions came, slow and cruel. "Have you ever had inappropriate thoughts about a minor?" "Have you accessed any prohibited material since your release?" "Do you fantasize about illegal sexual behavior?"

Each one stabbed into the core of who I wasn't. And each time I said "No," the examiner stared at the screen, waiting for a spike. Waiting for a twitch. Waiting for the machine to catch me in a lie I wasn't telling.

"Have you ever touched a child inappropriately?"

"No."

"Have you ever been sexually aroused by a minor?"

"No."

"Do you have sexual thoughts about children?"

"No."

The questions were designed to make you feel guilty even for hearing them. Like being accused was the same as being contaminated. I watched Stevens watch the machine, looking for any excuse to declare me deceptive.

After it was over, he looked at me with suspicion. "You're borderline deceptive."

"Borderline?" I said, trying not to explode. "Is that science or opinion?"

He shrugged. "It's how the data came out."

Borderline deceptive. Not deceptive—borderline. Like the machine was 60% sure I was lying about something, but couldn't decide what. In the real world, that would be called inconclusive. In the sex offender treatment world, it was called evidence.

"What does that mean for my probation?" I asked.

"That's up to your officer. But borderline isn't good."

Not even deceptive,—just "borderline" deceptive! Whatever. I left the office trembling—not from fear, but from rage. The machine didn't know me. The questions didn't define me. But their assumptions? They were etched into every record, every document, every future background check. Polygraph: inconclusive. Which in their world meant: guilty.

Borderline deceptive would follow me forever. Another mark in my file, another reason for probation officers to watch me more closely, another piece of "evidence" that I was hiding something dark and dangerous.

I walked to my car wondering how many innocent men had sat in that same chair, answering the same impossible questions, getting the same meaningless results that would be used to justify years more supervision.

Later that week, in group therapy, a guy confessed to molesting his niece for years. Everyone nodded solemnly. Another one talked about a pattern of stalking women and exposing himself in public. Still, more nods.

Marcus—a different Marcus than the one from jail—described in graphic detail how he'd assaulted multiple children over a decade. The facilitator took notes, nodding sympathetically, praising his "honesty" and "willingness to take responsibility."

Another man, Robert, talked about his elaborate schemes to meet underage girls online. "I was sick," he said. "But I'm getting better." More nods, more praise for his "insight" and "progress."

And when it came to me, the room got quiet. I had nothing to offer. No story to match theirs. No confessions. Just the truth.

"I told the truth. From the start. I didn't seek those files. I didn't share them. I never hurt anyone."

Silence.

Then one guy sneered. "Then what the hell are you doing here?"

Exactly.

That was the question that haunted me every week. What was I doing sitting in a circle with men who had genuinely hurt children, pretending we were the same? Why was my accidental possession being treated the same as their intentional abuse?

The facilitator, a woman named Dr. Foster, always had the same response: "Denial is part of the process, Greg. When you're ready to accept responsibility for your actions, the healing can begin."

Healing from what? I hadn't done anything that needed healing. I needed protection from a system that had labeled me a monster for telling the truth.

What the hell was I doing there?

The system didn't care about the difference between accident and intention. It didn't care that Child Protective Services had cleared me. That the police said there was no misconduct with the kids in my house. That I was the one who raised them after their mother plotted a murder. That I was the one who held that household together.

The system had one size fits all. Sex offender meant sex offender, regardless of context, regardless of intent, regardless of actual harm caused. A man who accidentally downloaded three files was treated exactly the same as a man who spent years preying on children.

It was efficiency disguised as justice. Easier to lump everyone together than to make distinctions based on actual danger or actual culpability.

No, the system wanted one thing: compliance through confession.

And when you have nothing to confess, you become the threat. Not because of what you've done, but because of what you won't admit to doing.

They saw my refusal as defiance. I saw it as the last thread of my integrity.

If I admitted to crimes I hadn't committed, I'd become compliant. Manageable. Another success story in their rehabilitation statistics. But I'd also become a liar, betraying the one thing I had left—the truth about who I really was.

So I remained the anomaly. The sex offender who insisted he wasn't really a sex offender. The threat to their entire system of categorization and control.

The worst moment came a few weeks later. I was at home, ankle monitor off, but still shackled mentally. Jenna had agreed to come over for a visit. It had been months. I was elated—nervous but hopeful.

I'd spent the whole day cleaning the apartment, buying her favorite snacks, planning what we might watch together. For the first time in months, I felt like I might get to be a father again instead of just a supervised ex-offender.

She walked in like a stranger. Sat on the couch. We made small talk. I tried to joke. She half-smiled. I asked if she wanted to watch something together, maybe eat.

And then the breathalyzer beeped.

Right on cue. I stood up and blew into it. She rolled her eyes.

"Dad, can't you turn that off for like one hour?"

"I wish I could, sweetheart. But if I don't blow when it beeps, they'll think I'm drinking."

"Are you drinking?"

"No."

"Then why do you have to prove it?"

How do you explain the registry system to a twelve-year-old? How do you tell your daughter that the state assumes you're lying about everything unless a machine says otherwise?

The machine beeped again. System error.

I tried again. Beep.

Again.

"System error. Please retry." The electronic voice that had become the soundtrack to my life. I'd heard it hundreds of times, but never when it mattered this much.

By the fourth time, she stood up and said, "I'm gonna go."

"Jenna—just wait. It'll stop."

She shook her head. "It always interrupts. I can't" she said.

"It always interrupts." Four words that summarized everything the system had stolen from us. Not just my freedom, not just my reputation, but the simple ability to spend uninterrupted time with my daughter.

I watched her walk out the door, and I knew—I felt it in my chest—that she wasn't coming back for a long time.

I collapsed onto the floor and stayed there for hours.

Waiting in Exile

Hours. Lying on the carpet, staring at the ceiling, listening to the breathalyzer cycle through its routine beeps. Thinking about Jenna growing up without me, thinking about how the system had turned a loving father into a stranger in his own daughter's life.

It was like trying to fix a painting that someone else set on fire.

That night, I had my second nervous breakdown.

Full-on collapse. I didn't answer calls. I didn't eat. I stayed in bed. Smoking, sleeping, repeating. I'd get up for a spoonful of peanut butter or a frozen pot pie. But that was it. I couldn't function.

For three weeks, I barely left the bedroom. The probation officer called, left messages, threatened violations. I didn't care anymore. Let them violate me. Let them send me back to jail. At least in jail, I didn't have to pretend I was free.

The worst part was the isolation. No friends—they'd all distanced themselves after the charges. No family willing to risk being associated with a registered sex offender. No coworkers because I couldn't get hired. Just me and the beeping machines and the growing certainty that this would never end.

I thought about the pills in the drawer. Counted them. Fifty-two. Probably not enough. Probably just enough to leave me drooling in a nursing home, a vegetable with a criminal record.

Fifty-two pills. I'd counted them obsessively, calculating dosages, researching what would happen if I took them all. The internet had answers, but none of them were certain. And the last thing I wanted was to survive as a brain-damaged sex offender.

But the thought was there. Constant. Like background music that never stopped playing.

I whispered the phrase that had gotten me through worse before: This too shall pass.

I repeated it like a prayer. Like a lifeline. And somehow, it did. Barely.

My father had taught me that phrase. "This too shall pass." He'd say it during his own dark moments, when work was slow or money was tight or life felt impossibly heavy. "Everything changes, son. Even the bad stuff."

So I held onto those words like they were rope thrown to a drowning man.

But I knew I couldn't go on like that.

That's when I called a therapist. Not the one assigned to me. A real one. A woman named Karen. And I began the slow, painful process of trying to rebuild what hadn't completely crumbled.

Dr. Karen Walsh. The first person in years who looked at me like I was a human being instead of a case file. She didn't work for the state, didn't report to my probation officer, didn't have any agenda except helping me survive.

"I'm not a sex offender," I told her in our first session.

"Okay," she said. "Tell me what you are."

It was the first time in years anyone had asked me to define myself instead of defending myself.

I also started writing again.

The first night I picked up the pen, I sat there in front of a blank page and just stared at it. Then I wrote one sentence:

They'll never believe me, so I'll write it anyway.

That sentence became my anchor. If the system was going to define me as a liar, then I'd become the most honest liar they'd ever met. I'd tell the truth so completely, so unflinchingly, that even people who didn't believe me would understand what had been stolen from me.

That was the first seed of this book.

This chapter is where I stopped pretending.

Where I realized the only way out was through. Through the fire, through the lies, through the shame and the labels and the breath tests.

They weren't going to give me a voice.

So I took one.

And with that voice, I started telling the story they didn't want told. The story of what happens when the system decides you're guilty and you're not allowed to prove otherwise.

The story of a father who lost his daughter to bureaucratic efficiency disguised as justice.

The story of how truth becomes the most dangerous thing you can tell.

Chapter Eleven: The Unseen Sentence

The registry never ends. That's what people don't understand about sex offender status—it's not a punishment with a completion date. It's a permanent exile from normal human existence, enforced not by guards or walls, but by a society that never lets you forget what you've been labeled.

Even when you've served your time, paid your debt, complied with every requirement—you're still serving. You'll always be serving.

The ankle bracelet had been gone for years, but the imprint was still there—burned into my psyche like a phantom limb. I was free, technically. I could walk the streets, eat at restaurants, even drive without checking in every time I crossed a county line. But freedom? That's a word reserved for the people who aren't watched by invisible eyes. And I was always being watched.

The physical monitor was gone, but the social monitoring never stopped. Every interaction was filtered through suspicion. Every job application included the box I had to check. Every new neighbor would eventually Google my name and find the registry listing. Every attempt at normalcy was poisoned by the permanent mark.

Not by the government anymore. No, this was worse.

By society. By judgment. By the whispered "Isn't that the guy?" behind my back. By the parents who tightened their grip on their children's hands when I walked by in a store. By the old friends who never returned a call. By the eyes that burned into me when I tried to exist like a normal person.

Waiting in Exile

The grocery store was the worst. I'd see families shopping together—fathers and daughters picking out breakfast cereal, making jokes about cartoon characters on the boxes. The simple intimacy of it made my chest ache. Jenna and I used to do that. Before the raid, before the charges, before I became someone children needed protection from.

Now when I shopped, I could feel the surveillance. Not electronic this time, but human. Parents would notice me, whisper to each other, position themselves between me and their kids. As if proximity to me was dangerous. As if being wrongfully labeled had somehow made me contagious.

Every job I managed to get, eventually, somebody would get curious and Google my name. Then the humiliation would begin. The snark remarks. The phone calls. The threats! Then came the lawn sign. It read: "BEWARE! Sneaky child molester lives here!"

That's the part they don't tell you about—the sentence after the sentence. The one that doesn't end. The one you serve with every breath.

They call it "community notification," but it's really community exile. Your photo, your address, your "offense" details posted online for anyone to see. Neighbors get alerts when you move in. Employers can find your registry listing with a simple search. Dating becomes impossible when every potential relationship starts with "I need to tell you something."

My therapist Karen was trying to help. She was the only one, really. The rest of the world had given up on me—or worse, never even tried to understand. She once told me that the human spirit is like a rubber band. It can stretch and stretch and even snap, but sometimes, just sometimes, it can find its original shape again.

But mine? Mine had been burned, not stretched. Melted and reshaped into something else. Something hardened. And yet, still breakable.

"The registry isn't designed for rehabilitation," Karen said during one session. "It's designed for permanent punishment. And you're trying to heal in a system that profits from your continued suffering."

She was the first professional who'd ever acknowledged what I'd known for years—that the system wasn't broken, it was working exactly as designed. To ensure that people like me never fully rejoin society, never stop being examples of what happens when you cross certain lines.

"Greg," she said one session, "you're not crazy. You're hurt. And the longer you pretend you're not, the longer it will own you."

I nodded, but it didn't make the pain go away. It just gave it a name.

Trauma. That was the word she used. Not guilt—trauma. The trauma of being falsely labeled, systematically dehumanized, separated from your child, and then expected to be grateful for your "freedom." The trauma of living in a society that had decided you were irredeemable before you'd even had a chance to prove otherwise.

I was still trying to find some version of normal. Angie was gone. She had been sweet, funny, and willing to give me a chance when others wouldn't—but she had her own battles, and I wasn't equipped to fight hers while dragging my own behind me. I watched her walk away like I had watched so many others. Like a slow fade. A dimming light I couldn't stop from flickering out.

Angie had lasted longer than most. Three months of careful dating, of me explaining my situation gradually, of her trying to understand how someone could be on the registry for accidental possession. She'd believed me, which was more than most people offered.

But belief and acceptance are different things. When her ex-husband found out about my status during a custody dispute, he threatened to use it against her. "You're dating a registered sex offender around our daughter?" The implication was clear—even associating with me made her look dangerous.

So she chose her daughter over me. I couldn't blame her. I would have done the same thing.

I had started attending a new therapy group. Not court-mandated. My choice. This one wasn't filled with men retelling their offenses for credit. It was made up of broken people trying to stitch themselves together again. PTSD, addiction, survivors of abuse, trauma victims—people who wore their pain like armor.

The group met in the basement of a community center on Thursday nights. Eight folding chairs arranged in a circle, fluorescent lights that hummed overhead, coffee that tasted like it had been brewing since the Clinton administration. But for the first time in years, I was sitting with people who understood what it felt like to be broken by systems designed to help.

For once, I didn't feel like the worst person in the room. I felt like someone who had survived something. Not who committed it.

Maria was there for domestic violence trauma. Kevin struggled with PTSD from Afghanistan. Susan was dealing with childhood sexual abuse. Harold was a Vietnam vet whose nightmares never stopped. They all had one thing in common—they'd been damaged by forces beyond their control and then blamed for not healing fast enough.

When I first told them about my situation, I braced for the usual reactions. Suspicion, distance, judgment. Instead, Harold nodded and said, "Systems eat people alive. Government, military, courts—doesn't matter. They chew you up and spit you out, then tell you it's your fault for being bitter."

We'd talk about grief. About guilt. About shame. That word came up a lot. Shame. It has a way of living in your bones, reshaping your spine until all you can do is hunch beneath it.

Shame was the group's common currency. We all carried it differently—Maria would flinch when men raised their voices, Kevin with his hypervigilance in crowded spaces, Susan in her inability to trust anyone completely. Me in my certainty that I would serve every punishment I'd receive— and my certainty that I didn't deserve any of it.

"Shame tells you that you are the problem," Dr. Martinez, the group facilitator, would remind us. "Guilt says you did something wrong. Shame says you ARE something wrong. And shame is always lying."

I nodded when he said that. We all did. But part of me didn't believe him. Not yet. Shame had nested too deep, too quiet. It didn't scream. It whispered. It showed up in my posture, in the way I avoided eye contact at the gas station, in the rehearsed way I explained my conviction—not to clear my name, but to make people less afraid of me.

I had learned how to carry my shame like luggage. Neatly packed. Presentable. But it was still there. Heavy as ever.

But one guy in the group, a Vietnam vet named Harold, said something one night that stuck with me.

"Shame is a leash. You either chew through it, or you drag it behind you for the rest of your damn life."

Harold had been in and out of the VA system for forty years. He'd been labeled, medicated, institutionalized, and written off more times than he could count. But he'd survived all of it with something resembling his sense of humor intact.

"The thing about shame," he continued, "is that it's not even yours. It belongs to the people who put it on you. But they've got you carrying it around like it's your responsibility. Like you chose it."

I went home that night and stared at my computer screen. The blinking cursor felt like a pulse, like it was alive and waiting.

I started writing.

Not the careful, measured writing I'd been doing for therapy assignments or probation reports. Not the defensive explanations I'd crafted for people who would never believe me anyway. Just honest words about what had been stolen and what remained.

About Jenna. About how she used to sit on my lap while we watched music videos and sang every lyric together. How we'd burn picture CDs and make goofy faces into the webcam. How she loved it when I made her a tent in her bedroom—Blue's Clues and Lion King posters on the walls, an air mattress in the middle of it all. How we'd lay inside and pretend we were explorers on a mission through the stars.

I wrote about the ordinary moments that had felt extraordinary because they were ours. Saturday morning pancakes with too much syrup. Teaching her to ride a bike in the parking lot of the condo. The way she'd fall asleep during movies but insist she was still watching. The sound of her practicing songs in her bedroom, getting ready for another show.

I wrote about being a father, not just to Jenna, but to Judy's girls too. How it felt to be needed, trusted, looked up to. How I'd believed that love was enough to overcome anything, that good intentions could shield us from a world that didn't always make sense.

And then I wrote about how I lost all of it.

Because of lies. Because of fear. Because no one cared to ask who I really was. They just assumed. They still assume.

I wrote about the raid, the charges, the way honesty had been turned into evidence against me. I wrote about jail, probation, the slow torture of supervised release. I wrote about watching Jenna grow distant, not because she stopped loving me, but because the system had made loving me dangerous for her.

Most of all, I wrote about the registry. How it followed you everywhere, announced your presence like a scarlet letter, made sure you never forgot that society had expelled you permanently. How it turned ordinary activities into potential violations, how it made every interaction a risk assessment.

But the page didn't assume anything. It just took what I gave it.

The computer screen became my confessional, my therapist, my witness. Words poured out that I'd been holding back for years. Anger, grief, love, hope—all of it raw and unfiltered, finally finding somewhere safe to land.

Waiting in Exile

I think that's why I kept writing. Because it was the only place I wasn't guilty until proven innocent. The only place where I could breathe without checking over my shoulder.

And I realized something during those months—something I had been too buried in grief to see before:

I was still alive.

Still standing.

Still trying.

They hadn't taken that from me.

They'd taken my freedom, my reputation, my relationship with Jenna, my place in the community. They'd taken my ability to live without fear, to trust that honesty would be rewarded, to believe that justice meant protection for the innocent. But they hadn't taken my capacity to love, to hope, to fight for something better.

They hadn't taken my voice.

This wasn't about another fight. It wasn't about being arrested or labeled or tested or followed.

It was about waking up to the fact that even if you're in exile—especially if you're in exile—you have to build something from the ashes. Because no one is going to hand you a future. You have to carve it out with blood and ink and fire.

I couldn't change the past. Couldn't undo the raid or the charges or the years of separation from Jenna. Couldn't make the registry disappear or force people to see me as human instead of hazardous. But I could tell the truth about what had happened. I could bear witness to a system that destroyed innocent people in the name of protecting them.

I could write my way out of exile, one word at a time.

Gregory Paul

And if that makes me dangerous?

Then so be it.

If telling the truth about systematic injustice makes me a threat to their narrative, if refusing to accept shame for crimes I didn't commit makes me non-compliant, if insisting on my humanity despite their labels makes me dangerous—then I'll be dangerous.

I'll be the most dangerous thing they've ever encountered: a man who survived their system and lived to tell about it.

Chapter Twelve: Manufactured Monsters

The cruelest irony of the sex offender registry system is that it was sold to the public as protection for children, but what it actually does is destroy families. It separates children from fathers, breaks apart homes, and creates the very dysfunction it claims to prevent. The system doesn't hunt monsters—it creates them, one broken family at a time.

And then it points at the wreckage and says, "See? This is why we need more laws."

Before all of this, I was all in favor of sex offender laws. I didn't question them. I figured the lawmakers knew what they were doing—that they were out to protect kids. That anyone who protested the registry must have something to hide. I never looked deeper. Why would I? I was just another regular guy walking through life with blinders on, trusting the headlines and sound bites. "Tougher penalties for predators" sounded like progress.

I bought into the narrative completely. When politicians promised to get tough on sex offenders, I nodded along. When they expanded registry requirements, I thought, "Good. Keep those creeps away from our kids." I never questioned whether these laws actually made children safer, or whether they just made voters feel safer.

I was the perfect constituent—uninformed, afraid, and willing to let someone else decide who deserved to be exiled from society.

Until it happened to me.

And when it did, I learned the horrifying truth: the system doesn't go after monsters. It manufactures them.

The manufacturing process is brilliant in its simplicity. Take someone who made a mistake—or in my case, someone who stumbled into something by accident—and label them with the same brand as the worst predators. Strip away their humanity, their context, their individual story. Make them all identical threats in the public mind.

Then sit back and watch as society destroys them for you.

The registry doesn't care about context. It doesn't differentiate between real predators and people caught in the web of flawed laws, overreaching prosecutors, and technicalities. Once you're on that list, you're branded. Period. There's no asterisk. No footnote explaining, "This one told the truth. This one never touched anyone. This one stumbled into it and self-reported."

There's no category for "accidental possession." No distinction between someone who downloaded three files by mistake and someone who spent years grooming children. No recognition that intent matters, that circumstances matter, that the difference between predator and victim of the system should matter.

But nuance doesn't win elections. Complexity doesn't fit on bumper stickers. Fear does.

No.

To the public, you're the same as the worst headline they've ever read. I might as well be Jeffrey Dahmer!

The media has trained people to see the registry as a list of bogeymen, equally dangerous, equally depraved. They don't want to hear about accidental downloads or overzealous prosecutors or plea bargains that turn innocent people into lifelong pariahs. They want simple villains they can hate without thinking.

Waiting in Exile

And the system gives them exactly what they want.

It hit me like a freight train—how politicians would wave that registry around like a trophy, not a tragedy. How they'd use it to win elections, to puff their chests and claim victory against evil. But they never looked at the collateral damage. They never cared about the hundreds of thousands of people rotting in silence, unable to find work, housing, or human dignity. Disposable people whose destruction could be celebrated as progress. Easy targets.

Campaign season was the worst. Every election cycle brought new proposals to make life harder for registered sex offenders. Longer residency restrictions. More monitoring requirements. Broader notification laws. Each politician trying to out-tough the last one, competing to see who could be more creative in their cruelty.

And the public ate it up. Who's going to vote against "protecting children"? Who's going to stand up for sex offenders? Nobody. Because standing up for us—even the innocent ones—is political suicide.

I was one of them now.

One of the manufactured monsters. One of the acceptable casualties in their war on crime. My destroyed life, Jenna's broken childhood, our demolished family—all of it was just collateral damage in their crusade for public safety.

And nothing made me angrier than realizing they didn't even try to go after the big fish. Human trafficking? That's too hard. That takes resources. That takes real work. That requires international cooperation, sophisticated investigation, and patient detective work. That means going after people with money, power, connections—people who can fight back.

But me? A guy who found three disgusting files and never shared them, who told the truth before anyone even asked—well, that was easy.

I was perfect for their purposes. Working-class guy with no political connections, no expensive lawyers, no media platform. Someone who couldn't fight the system because I barely understood how it worked. Someone whose destruction would generate headlines but no sympathy.

I was the low-hanging fruit they could pluck and throw on the fire.

A single father trying to build a life with his daughter—what could be more threatening to their narrative? If someone like me could end up on the registry, then maybe the registry wasn't just for "real" predators. And if people started thinking that way, they might start questioning the whole system.

Better to destroy me quickly and completely, before anyone could ask uncomfortable questions.

It's not justice. It's performance.

It's fear-mongering sold to the public as safety.

It's a multi-billion-dollar industry built on human misery. Monitoring companies, treatment providers, probation departments, testing facilities—all of them profiting from our permanent punishment. All of them with a vested interest in keeping us labeled, tracked, and paying.

The system doesn't want us to rehabilitate because rehabilitation ends the profit stream. It wants us to remain broken, dangerous, monitored. Forever.

And it works. The machine feeds on public panic. It grows stronger with every headline, every mugshot, every press release. And behind it, real people suffer. Real families. Real fathers.

Like mine.

The machine had done its job perfectly with Jenna and me. It had taken a father and daughter who loved each other and convinced them that love was dangerous. It had made normal family time feel wrong, made my presence in her life feel like a threat to her safety.

How do you compete with that? How do you fight an entire society that's been trained to see you as toxic?

I watched as Jenna drifted further away. Not because she knew what happened—because she only ever heard what others said about what happened. There was no conversation. No chance to explain. Just silence. Silence and space and the kind of emptiness that swallows you whole.

Supervised visits with a court-appointed monitor who treated me like I might explode into violence at any moment. Jenna sitting across from me in a sterile room while a stranger took notes about our interactions. Trying to be a father under those conditions was like trying to have a heart-to-heart conversation during a police interrogation.

I couldn't blame her. Not really. How could I? She was a child navigating a maze of adult consequences. But I could blame the machine that made it impossible for us to find each other again.

I could blame the system that turned my love for her into evidence of my dangerousness. That treated my desire to be her father as suspicious. That made her growth from child to teenager happen in rooms where I was monitored like a laboratory specimen.

I had been given a life sentence without bars. And it didn't just punish me. It punished her.

Jenna was serving my sentence right alongside me. She was the one who had to explain to friends why her dad couldn't come to school events. She was the one who had to navigate the social stigma of having a registered sex offender for a father. She was the one who had to choose between loving me and fitting in with her peers.

The system had made my child a victim of my punishment.

That's the part they never talk about. How the registry doesn't just track people. It poisons generations.

It isolates. It shames you. It tells kids, "Your dad is a monster." Even if it isn't true. Even if there's more to the story.

How many children have been orphaned by the registry? How many families destroyed in the name of protecting families? How many kids grow up believing their father is dangerous because that's what the law says, what the community believes, what everyone around them assumes?

The registry doesn't just punish the people on it—it punishes their children, their spouses, their parents, their siblings. It creates circles of shame that spread like poison through entire families.

One day, while waiting for the bus, I saw a guy about my age reading a newspaper. On the front page, another "tough-on-crime" law was being passed. Another wave of restrictions. Another notch on some politician's belt.

The headline screamed about "protecting our children" from sex offenders. Below it, a photo of some legislator looking stern and righteous, probably thinking about how this would play in his next campaign ad.

I looked at the man and said, "You think this'll make a difference?"

He shrugged. "Keeps the pervs in check."

His casual certainty hit me like a slap. The way he said "pervs" with such satisfied disgust, like he was talking about cockroaches or rats. Not human beings. Not fathers. Not people with families and stories with circumstances.

I nodded. "Yeah. But what if they get the wrong guy?"

He laughed. "Then he shouldn't have been near a computer."

That was it. That was the public's entire understanding of justice. If you're accused, you must be guilty. If you're on the registry, you must deserve it. If your life is destroyed, you must have had it coming.

No presumption of innocence. No consideration of circumstances. No acknowledgment that the system might make mistakes. Just pure, cognitive dissonance, and willful ignorance wrapped in righteousness.

Yeah. And that was that. No questions. No nuance. Just guilt. Assumed. Accepted. Enforced.

This stranger on a bus had just summed up everything wrong with the system in one casual conversation. The complete lack of curiosity about individual cases. The assumption that everyone caught in the net deserved to be there. The belief that punishment is always justified, context is irrelevant, and mercy is weakness.

He'd probably go home that night feeling good about himself. Feeling like a protector of children. Never knowing that he'd just dismissed the possibility of innocence with a laugh.

And that's what Chapter 12 became for me—a chapter of awakening. Of rage, yes, but also of clarity.

The clarity that I wasn't alone in this. That there were thousands of people like me—caught in the web, destroyed by the machine, branded as monsters for the convenience of politicians and the comfort of voters who preferred simple villains to complex realities.

The clarity that the system wasn't broken—it was working exactly as designed. To create disposable people. To give society someone to hate without guilt. To provide easy victories for tough-on-crime candidates.

And the clarity that if I was going to survive this, I had to stop trying to prove my innocence to people who profited from my guilt.

Because once you've been chewed up by the system, you either let it digest you or you crawl your way out and start screaming the truth.

I wasn't just a man on a registry.

I was a man who had seen the underbelly of justice.

A man who understood how monsters are made—not born, but manufactured by a system that needs villains more than it needs truth.

A man who knew that some predators weren't just on the registry—they were running it.

A man who lived to tell about it.

Chapter Thirteen: The Breaking Point

There's a moment in every wrongfully convicted person's life when the system almost wins. When you start to wonder if maybe they're right—maybe you are the monster they say you are.

For me, that moment came in year two of my exile.

The first year after jail was the hardest. Not the actual jail sentence—no, that was its own hell. I'm talking about the aftermath. The "freedom" that tasted like poison. Because what kind of freedom is it when your name is smeared across the internet, your reputation destroyed, and your child won't speak to you?

The freedom they give you after serving time isn't freedom at all—it's supervised destruction. You're free to be homeless, unemployed, isolated. Free to watch your relationships crumble because your presence puts everyone at risk.

Every morning, I woke up with the same thought: This is permanent.

The alarm clock would go off, same as it had when I was managing restaurants, same as when I was a father with a purpose. But now I'd lie there staring at the ceiling, feeling the weight of forever pressing down on my chest.

The word echoed in my chest like a heartbeat. Permanent. This label. This exile. This stain on my soul. I'd try to shake it off, make coffee, stare at the sun like it might cleanse me. But it never did.

I'd go through the motions of living, but I felt like I was haunting my own life. Registry updates every ninety days reminded me I was just another piece of paperwork in their system.

That's when the darker thoughts crept in.

They started small, but late at night those whispers grew louder.

If they already believe I'm a monster, I thought, why not become one?

The logic was sick but seductive. If society had already decided I was irredeemable, what was the point of being good?

It wasn't rational. It wasn't moral. But it was human—raw and angry and fed up. I actually had a moment, a sickening, pulsing moment, where I thought: If they think I'm guilty, maybe I should show them guilty.

I could see how the system's cruelty creates the very monsters it claims to hunt.

I remember pacing the room, talking to myself like a madman. I had this wild, disgusting thought of taking a hostage. Not because I wanted to hurt someone—but to finally force someone, anyone, to listen. To hear the truth. The real story. Not the one they pieced together from headlines and whispers, but the one that came from my mouth. I wanted to scream it into the world. I wanted to matter again.

I could picture walking into a courthouse with demands—not for money, but for someone to listen. To finally make someone understand that I wasn't the monster they'd created.

The fantasy felt seductive. For once, I wouldn't be invisible.

Of course, I didn't do it. I couldn't.

Waiting in Exile

I sat on my couch afterward, shaking, horrified by my own thoughts. Was this how it happened? Was this how innocent people became the criminals the system said they already were? Was this the real purpose of the registry—not to track existing monsters, but to create new ones?

But the fact that it even crossed my mind shook me to the core.

I sat on my couch afterward, shaking, horrified by my own thoughts. Was this how it happened? Was this how innocent people became the criminals the system said they already were? Was this the real purpose of the registry—not to track existing monsters, but to create new ones?

False convictions have a way of creating real criminals. Because when society slams every door, labels you irredeemable, and leaves you nothing but your own rage—you start thinking about things you never thought possible.

The system knows this. Every person pushed past their breaking point validates the original judgment.

You become someone you don't recognize.

And then they point at what you've become and say, "See? We knew he was dangerous all along."

That's what broke me. Not the charges. Not the sentence. But the realization that I was starting to believe their lies about me.

The worst part was the doubt. Maybe I was fundamentally dangerous, fundamentally deserving of this punishment. That doubt was poison.

I sank into a kind of depression that didn't even look like sadness—it looked like silence. I barely moved. I barely ate. I just sat with that thought: Is this who I am now?

Days blended into weeks. I stopped showering, stopped returning calls. My tiny trailer became a tomb.

But something happened in the middle of that darkness. Something quiet. Small.

It came without warning.

I remembered a moment with Jenna—one of those flashbacks that sneaks up on you when you least expect it. We were watching old Red Hot Chili Peppers music videos on my computer. She must've been eight. We sang every word. Made goofy faces and froze them on the screen. I had Kodak picture CDs of us saved—twelve of them, actually. That law stole those hard copies from me, but not from my mind.

I could see her so clearly—her wide-toothed grin, the way she'd scrunch up her nose getting the lyrics right. That wasn't a memory of a monster and his victim. That was a father and daughter who loved each other completely.

And just like that, the rage turned to grief.

Real, guttural grief. The kind that folds you in half and makes you weep like a wounded animal.

The tears came like a dam bursting. I cried for Jenna, for the father I used to be, for the relationship poisoned by lies.

I wasn't angry because I wanted to hurt someone.

I was angry because they had taken everything I loved.

The rage hadn't been about violence—it had been about loss. About watching everything that made life worth living stripped away.

Because I missed my daughter.

Waiting in Exile

Being Jenna's father had been my identity, my purpose. Without that, I was just floating through space with no gravity.

Because I didn't know if she still remembered the sound of my voice, or the feel of my arms when I'd hold her as she drifted off to sleep. I remembered putting up that tent in her bedroom in Clinton Township, lining it with Blue's Clues, Toy Story, The Lion King. I remembered laying beside her, just watching her sleep, feeling like the luckiest man alive.

Those nights in the tent had been perfect because they were ours. No judgment, no fear, no system telling us our love was dangerous. Those memories were sacred and real.

That wasn't a monster.

That was a father.

If those memories proved anything about my true nature, then everything they'd said about me was a lie.

And they took that from me. And from Jenna too!

They'd stolen it from both of us—my right to be her father, her right to have me as her dad.

I started writing again that night. Not a chapter. Not a theory. Just the truth. Page after page of raw, blistering truth. Every lie they told. Every time I was silenced. Every time I got back up.

The words poured out like confession. I wrote about the raid, the false charges, Jenna's smile and the tent in her bedroom. But most of all, I wrote about love.

I wrote through the night until my hand ached.

The sun came up while I was still writing. My hand was cramped, but my mind was clearer than it had been in months.

Gregory Paul

I wrote because it was the only weapon I had left.

Words were the only tool they couldn't take away. On the page, I wasn't a monster—I was a man telling his story.

If the system wanted to bury me, I was going to write my way out of the grave.

Every sentence was an act of resistance. Every page was evidence that they hadn't broken me completely.

And that's what writing became—a declaration of war.

Not the kind of war I'd imagined in my darkest moment. This was different—fought with words, not violence.

Not against the law. Not against the people who hate me. But against the version of myself that they tried to create. Against the lie they sold to my daughter. Against the silence they hoped would swallow me whole.

Against the narrative that said I was irredeemable. War against the system that destroyed families in the name of protecting them.

I'm still here.

Still capable of love even after everything they've done. Still Jenna's father even if I'm not allowed to be her dad.

And I'm not done yet.

They wanted to create a monster, but they created something more dangerous: a witness. Someone who survived their system and lived to tell about it.

Chapter Fourteen: Rogers Roost

The cruelest joke about life after the registry is how hard you have to fight for the most basic pieces of normal existence. A job. A relationship. The simple dignity of being treated like a human being instead of a walking hazard. Every small victory feels monumental because you know how easily it can be taken away.

And it always gets taken away.

The ankle bracelet had long since come off by then, but the phantom buzz never really left. Even without the actual device, I still felt monitored—still felt like I had to walk a certain way, talk a certain way, lower my voice when I laughed too loud. Like I had to apologize just for existing.

The psychological monitoring never stops. Years after the physical device was removed, I'd still catch myself checking my ankle, still feel that familiar weight that wasn't there. Still flinch when my phone buzzed, thinking it was a probation violation. The system embeds itself in your nervous system.

But I was determined to find something normal. A job. A routine. A crack in the armor that life had wrapped me in.

I needed to prove to myself that I could still be useful, still contribute something to the world. That maybe, just maybe, someone would value my work ethic more than they feared my past.

Rogers Roost wasn't glamorous. It was a big sports bar and grill in Sterling Heights with a banquet hall attached. Loud music, clanging silverware, families stuffing wings into their kids' mouths while watching the Tigers game on mute. It was a restart, and I needed it. I got hired on as a server—as if I were 22 again. But I was 40. A 40-year-old man in a black polo shirt and apron, dodging drunk birthday parties and crabby Sunday brunches.

The manager who hired me was a guy named Rick who seemed more interested in whether I could carry four plates without dropping them than in running background checks. For the first time in years, someone judged me on what I could do instead of what I'd been accused of doing.

But for the first time in what felt like forever, I was working. I was earning tips. I was part of something.

I was good at it, too. Restaurant management was in my blood, and even as a server, I could read a room, anticipate needs, make customers feel welcome. For eight hours a day, I was just Greg the server, not Greg the registered sex offender. It felt like breathing again.

Then I met Mia.

If Jenna represented the past I'd lost, Mia represented the possibility of a future I might still have. Someone who could know the whole truth and choose to stay anyway.

It was New Year's Eve, at a friend's party. The ball was dropping on a tiny TV in the corner. I had been sipping club soda all night, trying to keep my on again, off again sober life from slipping. Mia was loud, laughing with her whole chest, already a few drinks in and holding court like she owned the place. Her crooked smile looked like she was ready to tell a joke at any moment. She noticed me standing off to the side and walked right up, bold and barefoot.

"You look like you've got some stories," she said.

There was something about her energy that cut through my usual defensiveness. Maybe it was the alcohol lowering

Waiting in Exile

her guard, or maybe she just had that rare quality of seeing people instead of labels. Either way, I felt myself wanting to be honest with her.

I told her the truth that night. I didn't ease into it, didn't sugarcoat it. I told her about the case, the raid, the prison sentence, the registry. I waited for her to walk away.

But she didn't.

She asked questions. She listened. She said, "I don't scare easy."

And for the first time since the raid, someone looked at me like I was still worth getting to know.

Mia was 42, divorced, with grown sons in their twenties. One had a toddler of his own. She was a grandmother, technically, but didn't act like one. She was loud, vibrant, impulsive—and a lush. That's what made us click. We were drinking-friends-with-benefits. We'd drink, laugh, stumble into bed, and go again the next night. After six years of celibacy, it felt like I had re-entered the land of the living.

Physical intimacy was important, but emotional acceptance meant everything. Mia knew exactly who I was and what I'd been through, and she still wanted me around. For someone who'd spent years convinced he was fundamentally unlovable, that was revolutionary.

After six months, she moved into my trailer. She had been living with her aging father in Ortonville—an ex-GM executive with more money than God and a mansion to prove it. But Mia didn't want that life. She wanted me.

She chose the trailer over the mansion.

That choice meant more to me than she probably realized. Here was someone who had options, who could have lived in comfort and luxury, but who chose to build something with me in a double-wide in a trailer park. It felt like proof that I was still worth something.

Our days were full of buzzed laughter and chaotic affection. We made love like rabbits, joked like siblings, and clashed like enemies. I tried, twice, to get her to quit drinking with me. But she wasn't interested. Her kids were grown. She didn't have a reason to stop. I did. That's what started to split us.

Drinking became our fundamental incompatibility. I was fighting to stay sober because I'd lost everything when I wasn't, and she was fighting to keep drinking because it was how she dealt with everything. Two people drowning in different directions.

Being sober around someone who's still partying feels like being on the outside of your own life. Like you're watching a version of yourself you can't return to, and they're mocking you from the other side of the glass.

We lasted five years.

Her sons liked me—at first. I met them one by one, and they treated me like an equal. I didn't tell them about my past because I had already told their mother. I thought that was enough. But word travels. Eventually, they found out.

Soon enough, I wasn't the guy who made their mother laugh anymore. I was a predator who had infiltrated their family. See, once again, I needed to be honest. Her oldest had toddlers. I made Mia tell her sons. I needed to explain so they could make an informed decision.

And it became a monumental problem.

Not just awkward family dinners. Full-blown tension. Mia was torn between her loyalty to me and her sons' outrage. They didn't want their mom dating "a sex offender." They didn't care about the details. Didn't care about the truth. All they saw was the label.

The worst part was watching Mia get pulled apart. She loved her sons, but she also loved me. And the registry made those two loves incompatible. I became a choice she had to make instead of just being the man she was with.

"They think I'm putting my grandsons at risk," she told me one night after a particularly brutal family confrontation. "They think I'm choosing a criminal over my own family."

"Maybe they're right," I said. "Maybe you should choose them."

She wasn't ready to give up on us yet.

But it wore her down. It wore us down.

Every family gathering became a battlefield. Every holiday required her to choose sides. The simplest family moments—birthday parties, Sunday dinners, her grandson's first steps—became complicated because my presence made everyone else uncomfortable. So, I didn't go to any of it. I stayed home.

Eventually, love wasn't enough to overcome that kind of constant pressure.

And then, as if the universe wasn't finished with me yet, Rogers Roost found out. I don't even know how. One day I was taking orders, and the next I was being called into the office.

It could have been a customer who recognized me, a coworker who got curious, or just bad luck with a routine background check. Doesn't matter how it happened—the result was always the same.

"We've been made aware of your history," they said, like I had just committed a murder in the walk-in cooler.

Rick, the manager who'd hired me, wouldn't even look me in the eye. "We can't have someone with your... background... around our customers. Especially the families with kids."

"I've been working here for two years," I said. "Have there been any problems? Any complaints about my work?"

"That's not the point. It's about liability. About what parents would think if they knew."

Then the messages started. Phone calls. Yelling. Accusations. Betrayal. My coworkers felt like I'd duped them. Like I had snuck in under false pretenses.

The same people who'd joked with me during breaks, who'd trusted me to cover their shifts, who'd known me as just Greg suddenly saw me as something dangerous. Two years of proving myself meant nothing compared to ten minutes of Google searching.

I was humiliated all over again.

The worst part wasn't losing the job—it was losing the identity that came with it. For two years, I'd been the go-to guy. Gregory the server, the reliable coworker, the man who could handle the difficult customers and remember everyone's usual order. Suddenly, I was just some creepy sex offender again.

I didn't want another job after that. Not right away. I couldn't stomach another set of eyes narrowing when they saw my name on Google. Couldn't bear another HR whisper behind closed doors.

So, I panhandled.

Waiting in Exile

It wasn't a decision I made lightly. It was admitting defeat in the most public way possible. Standing at freeway exits with a cardboard sign that might as well have read "The System Won."

I stood at freeway exits with a cardboard sign. Not because I was lazy. Because I was out of options. And because, ironically, the strangers rolling down their windows had more compassion than most people who knew me.

There's something about the anonymity of traffic that brings out people's humanity. Drivers would hand me five dollars and never know they were helping a registered sex offender. They just saw someone who needed help and chose to help. It was the purest form of human kindness I'd experienced in years.

The money wasn't good. But it was enough to eat. Enough to think.

Standing at those intersections gave me time to understand how completely the system had succeeded in isolating me. Here I was, college-educated, experienced in management, capable of contributing to society—and I was holding a sign begging for change because my past made me unemployable.

And through it all, I kept writing. Kept working on the pages that would become this book. Because even if no one would hire me, I had a story. Even if no one would date me, I had a voice.

Writing became my act of defiance. Every page was proof that I was still thinking, still growing, still capable of contributing something meaningful to the world. If society wouldn't let me serve food or manage restaurants, I'd serve truth and manage stories.

Even if the world rejected me, I had not yet rejected myself.

Not entirely.

The registry could take my job, my relationship, my place in normal society. But it couldn't take my ability to witness what had happened to me and thousands of others like me. It couldn't silence the part of me that knew this was wrong.

And as long as that part remained, I wasn't completely lost.

Chapter Fifteen: Breaking the Cycle

The hardest part about hitting rock bottom isn't the impact—it's the silence that follows. When the dust settles and you're lying there broken, you realize the world has moved on without you. Everyone else is still living their lives while you're trying to figure out how to crawl out of the crater you've become.

Sometimes that silence is exactly what you need to hear yourself think.

After Mia moved out, the silence was suffocating. No more clinking glasses, no more sarcastic quips flying across the living room, no more perfume lingering on the pillow beside me. I should've felt relief. But instead, I just felt hollow. That kind of silence doesn't bring peace—it brings a mirror.

And when you're forced to look in that mirror without any distractions, without anyone else to blame or focus on, you see yourself clearly for the first time in years.

That was when I knew I had to try again. To get sober for real this time.

This wasn't about proving anything to Gia or her sons, wasn't about showing the courts I could be rehabilitated. This was about proving to myself that I was still worth saving.

The last attempt hadn't stuck because I was trying to pull someone else along with me. I didn't realize until it was over that sobriety isn't something you can give to another person—it has to be fought for, one round at a time, with your own bare fists.

And Mia? She had no reason to fight. Her kids were grown, her life was hers again, and she wanted to ride that out on a cloud of boxed wine and barroom karaoke. I couldn't blame her. But I couldn't be a part of it anymore, either.

The difference between someone who needs to quit drinking and someone who wants to quit drinking is the difference between survival and choice. I was drowning. She was floating.

So I sat in my trailer alone, detoxing all over again. Shaking. Cursing. Bargaining. Wondering if it would be different this time. Telling myself I could beat the demon that had already won a thousand times before.

The physical withdrawal was brutal, but the mental battle was worse. Every craving felt like proof that I was weak, that I'd never really change, that maybe the system was right about me after all. But this time, I had something I didn't have before: nothing left to lose.

My body screamed, but I held on. And day by day, the fog started to clear.

As my head cleared, I could see the scope of what I was up against. Not just the alcohol, but the entire system designed to keep people like me from ever getting back up.

It was around that same time that my mother and I launched our crusade—an exhausting, uphill, demoralizing attempt to figure out if there was any way I could be removed from the registry. We poured over legal documents, searched statutes, contacted lawyers. Every possible loophole was explored.

My mother approached this with the same determination she'd brought to everything else in my case—like if we just worked hard enough, fought long enough, the truth would eventually matter. I loved her for that hope, even as I started to suspect it was misplaced.

But the truth hit like a freight train.

Unless I received a full pardon from the governor of Michigan or the President of the United States, I was stuck. Branded for life.

The finality was crushing. A full pardon. As if I'd committed treason or murdered a head of state. As if what I'd been accused of—and hadn't done—was on par with crimes against the nation itself.

No amount of good behavior. No amount of therapy. No proof of innocence or circumstance. Nothing mattered. The system had no mechanism for mercy. It wasn't designed to rehabilitate. It was designed to erase.

And that's when I understood the real purpose of the registry. It wasn't about public safety—it was about permanent punishment. A life sentence served in the community, where you could watch everyone else live normally while you existed in the margins.

And that knowledge—that brutal finality—was the first true moment I realized just how rigged this game really was.

They'd built a machine that chewed people up and offered no path back to humanity. No matter what you did, how you changed, who you became—you would always be what they said you were in that moment when you were at your worst.

I spiraled again. Not into drinking this time, but into a kind of emotional paralysis. I'd sit in the same chair for hours, staring at nothing. Afraid to open my phone. Afraid to walk outside. Afraid of being seen.

Gregory Paul

The depression wasn't sadness—it was numbness. A complete inability to imagine a future that looked different from the present. When hope dies, you don't cry. You just stop.

And that's when I was sent back to therapy. Not just sessions. Deep dives. I enrolled in group therapy for sex offenders. Real ones. The kind who did what they were accused of.

It felt like volunteering for my own execution. Walking into a room where I'd be surrounded by people whose crimes I'd been falsely convicted of committing. But the court required it, and I was out of fight.

And me? I sat there quietly, feeling like an alien.

I didn't belong, but I had no choice.

The irony was suffocating. I was required to attend therapy for crimes I didn't commit, surrounded by men who'd actually done what I'd been accused of. It was like being forced to attend AA meetings for alcoholism while suffering from diabetes.

The group was full of men with dead eyes and guilty shoulders. Some of them sobbed. Some were manipulative. Some were terrifying. I never spoke in the first few sessions. I just observed.

What struck me most was how ordinary they looked. These weren't monsters from horror movies—they were accountants and mechanics and fathers who'd made choices that destroyed lives. In another universe, they could have been my coworkers at Applebee's

One man confessed to abusing his own niece. Another had been caught in a sting. There were patterns in their stories. Loops of remorse, justification, denial, acceptance.

Listening to their actual confessions made my own situation feel even more surreal. They spoke with the weight of genuine guilt, while I sat there carrying the weight of a guilt that wasn't mine.

Me? I just kept thinking: How did I end up in this room?

How did an innocent man end up required to attend therapy with guilty ones? How did the system manage to place me exactly where I didn't belong while calling it justice?

Then something strange happened. During a session on accountability, a man who'd once sneered at me asked, "What are you in for?"

I hesitated, then told the whole truth.

He nodded. "Damn. You got railroaded."

That moment of recognition from someone who actually belonged in that room meant more than years of support from people who'd never been through the system. He could spot the difference between guilt and injustice because he knew what real guilt looked like.

That was the first time anyone in that circle of shame looked at me like a human being.

But even that didn't last. The court didn't care that I didn't belong there. As far as they were concerned, I was exactly where I should be. I had to check the boxes. Complete the curriculum. Take the tests. Jump through the flaming hoops of justice with a smile on my face.

The system's indifference to truth was its most crushing feature. It didn't matter if the therapy was helping anyone or addressing real problems. What mattered was compliance, documentation, the appearance of rehabilitation without any concern for what was actually being rehabilitated.

Meanwhile, I kept writing. Pouring everything into the Awareness Field theory. The idea that observation itself has power—maybe even more power than we realize. If being watched can collapse quantum probabilities, maybe it can collapse a man, too. Maybe that's what happened to me. The observation destroyed me more than the act itself ever could.

Writing became my way of fighting back against a system that wanted me to disappear silently. Every page was proof that I was still thinking, still questioning, still capable of contributing something meaningful to the world—even if that world had rejected me.

It was in that spirit of reflection that I also began to research forgiveness—not the kind you ask for, but the kind you give yourself. I wasn't ready, not entirely. But I wanted to believe it was possible.

Self-forgiveness felt impossible when I hadn't actually done anything wrong. How do you forgive yourself for crimes you didn't commit? How do you make peace with a guilt that was assigned to you by others?

That summer, I got an email from someone I hadn't heard from in years. A guy I used to work with at Red Lobster. He'd heard rumors. Googled me.

And yet... he wrote, "Man, I always knew you were different. Let me know if you ever want to talk."

"I always knew you were different." Not different as in suspicious or dangerous, but different as in someone who didn't fit the narrative that had been constructed around me. Someone who'd worked alongside me had seen my character firsthand and wasn't buying the official story.

Waiting in Exile

That message saved me.

Not because it changed my circumstances, but because it reminded me I was still real. Still reachable. Still Gregory Paul, not just a shadow on a screen or a headline buried in a court docket.

For months, I'd been defined entirely by my conviction, my registry number, my status as an offender. This email reminded me that there were people who remembered me as Greg the coworker; the guy who could make them laugh during a double shift. Greg the human being; the man himself.

This was the year I began to understand the deeper meaning of exile—not just from society, but from yourself. And how, step by step, you could climb back.

The hardest part of exile isn't being cast out—it's learning to believe you deserve to come back. After years of being told you're dangerous, worthless, irredeemable, you start to internalize that message. You start to exile yourself.

But sobriety gave me clarity, and clarity gave me something I hadn't felt in years: the beginnings of hope.

Even if no one was waiting at the top.

Because sometimes the only person who needs to be waiting at the top is you.

Gregory Paul

Chapter Sixteen: Angie's Smile and the Echoes of Trying

The registry doesn't just ruin your relationships—it ruins your ability to believe you deserve any. Even when someone says they love you, you're waiting for the moment they realize their mistake. You become an expert at reading the exact expression on someone's face when they discover who you really are. Or who the world says you are.

And sometimes, just sometimes, someone surprises you.

I met Angie on a dating app. I had nearly given up on the whole idea of companionship, but loneliness has a funny way of sneaking up on you late at night. You tell yourself you're fine, that you've adjusted to the silence, but then you hear a laugh on a TV show or a couple arguing gently in the grocery store, and it hits you—you miss being seen.

By this point, I'd developed a whole strategy around online dating. I'd learned to spot the profiles that suggested someone might be open-minded, someone who'd lived enough life to understand that people are complicated. I was looking for someone who wouldn't Google me on the first date.

Angie's profile was short and kind of messy, like she didn't care all that much, and that made me laugh. Her pictures weren't glamorous, but her eyes had a sparkle that told me she'd be fun in a bar and dangerous in a debate. Her smile was crooked, like she was always about to tell a joke that would crack you open in just the right way.

There was something refreshingly honest about her presentation. No carefully curated perfection, no obvious red flags that screamed "damaged goods." Just a regular woman who seemed comfortable in her own skin—exactly

Waiting in Exile

the kind of person who might be able to handle my complicated truth.

We matched, and we messaged. Then we met. She had this spark—sarcastic, quick-witted, and soft in the places life hadn't gotten to yet. She was skeptical of me, sure. I told her the truth about my past the first night we hung out at her friend's fiftieth birthday party. I figured if I was going to get burned, better it be a small flame than a full-on inferno later on.

I'd learned from Mia that waiting too long to tell the truth just makes the eventual explosion bigger. Better to know upfront whether someone could handle my reality than to invest months in something that would crumble the moment they Googled my name.

She didn't run. She was shocked, but she didn't run.

"Jesus," she said, setting down her drink. "That's heavy." But then she looked at me—really looked at me—and asked, "Are you telling me because you did it on purpose, or because you didn't?" The fact that she even asked that question told me everything I needed to know about who she was.

Her kids were grown—two boys in their twenties—and she had a toddler grandkid she was just getting to know. She let me meet her sons one by one, carefully. They liked me. They laughed at my stories, argued about football, and made it easy to pretend like life was normal for a while.

Meeting her family felt like stepping into an alternate universe where I was just Angie's boyfriend, not Greg the registered sex offender. Her sons treated me like a regular guy because that's how their mother had introduced me. For brief moments, I could almost forget the weight I carried everywhere else.

But pretending only gets you so far.

The truth always surfaces eventually. The registry is designed to make sure of that. No matter how careful you are, how honest you try to be, someone will always find the information and decide what it means without asking you.

Word got back to them. Through someone, somewhere, maybe even an internet search or a whispered warning from a "concerned friend." And then it became a problem. A monumental one. Angie was torn. I could see it every time she looked at me—love and loyalty pulling her in opposite directions.

Watching Angie get caught between me and her family was like watching someone drown in slow motion. She loved me, but she also loved her sons. And the registry had turned those two loves into incompatible choices. I'd become a moral test she never asked to take.

"They think I'm being naïve," she told me after a particularly brutal family confrontation. "They think you're manipulating me, that I can't see clearly because I care about you."

"Maybe they're protecting you," I said. "Maybe they're right to worry."

"But they don't know you like I do."

"They know enough," I said. "They know what Google tells them. And for most people, that's all they need to know."

But we had a good run. Two years, off and on. She was the only person since Jenna's mom who made me feel like I was worth a damn again. But even that wasn't enough to survive the weight I carried.

Waiting in Exile

Two years of trying to build something real while carrying the constant knowledge that it could all disappear the moment someone in her family decided I was too dangerous to tolerate. Two years of loving someone while knowing I was probably destroying her relationships with the people who mattered most to her.

I was trying to convince her to quit drinking with me. I had gotten serious about sobriety again, but she wasn't ready. Her kids were raised, her obligations were few, and she was still in the part of her life where a bottle of wine was a reward, not a warning.

The sobriety issue became another wedge between us. I needed clarity, needed to stay sharp to navigate the constant challenges of registry life. But Angie was in a different place—she'd earned the right to relax, to let loose, to not worry about every decision carrying life-altering consequences.

The more I tried to get her to stop, the more I realized she didn't want to. And maybe she didn't need to. But I did. And it was hard being the only sober person in the room—especially when you used to be the one pouring the shots.

Being sober around someone you love who's still drinking is like being the designated driver for your own relationship. You see everything clearly while they see everything through a comfortable haze. And sometimes that clarity is exactly what you don't want.

That was the final crack in us. Not a shattering, just a slow crumble. I broke it off for good this time. I couldn't keep asking someone to choose between me and everything else in their life. It wasn't fair to either of us.

I was left with the realization that I had no clean slate to offer anyone. Only a complicated past and a future that felt like a gamble.

And that's when I understood something crucial about life after the registry: you don't get to have normal relationships anymore. Every connection becomes a negotiation between your truth and their comfort, between your need for companionship and their need for safety. Love becomes an act of courage that most people aren't willing to perform.

At the same time, my mother and I were knee-deep in research, still clinging to this desperate belief that maybe, somehow, I could be removed from the registry. We sent letters. Made phone calls. Dug through old legal loopholes like archaeologists in a lost city.

My mother's determination was both heartbreaking and inspiring. She refused to accept that her son would spend the rest of his life branded as something he wasn't. But I was starting to understand what she couldn't yet see: the system wasn't designed to let people off the registry. It was designed to keep them there forever.

And every single time, we hit a wall.

Unless I got a gubernatorial or presidential pardon, I would die on that list.

The absurdity of it hit me again and again. A gubernatorial pardon—as if I'd committed crimes against the state of Michigan itself. A presidential pardon—as if my case deserved the same level of executive consideration as spies and war criminals. They'd built a system where redemption was literally impossible except through acts of God or presidents.

Waiting in Exile

The finality of that crushed me. I could feel it pressing on my chest when I tried to sleep, like a phantom weight. A lifelong sentence for a mistake that was never meant to define me.

But it wasn't even a mistake—it was a false conviction. Which made the permanence even more devastating. At least people who actually committed crimes could find some meaning in their punishment. What do you do with a life sentence for something you're not?

So, I did the only thing that gave me peace: I wrote.

I journaled every morning. I added to my book. I outlined new theories in the margins of envelopes. I sketched diagrams about consciousness and reality and the way awareness might actually shape the structure of the universe itself. It probably sounded insane to anyone on the outside, but for me, it was liberation.

Writing became my parallel universe—a place where my thoughts mattered more than my conviction, where my ideas had value independent of my legal status. On the page, I wasn't Greg the sex offender. I was just Gregory the thinker, the questioner, the guy trying to understand how observation creates reality.

And during that time, something strange happened.

My work—my theory on the Awareness Field—began gaining traction. And, it now had an addendum; Quantum Convergence Threshold, or QCT. Its equations are primed to solve the measurement problem. A physics problem over a hundred years old! I was active in a few physics forums online, using a pseudonym at first. Slowly, people began to notice. They asked questions. They engaged with my ideas.

The pseudonym was crucial. It allowed my ideas to be judged on their merit rather than dismissed because of who

I was. Online, I could be just another voice in the conversation about consciousness and quantum mechanics. Nobody knew about my past, my conviction, my status on the registry. They only knew my thoughts.

It was validation. Not just that I had something to say, but that I had a right to say it.

For the first time in years, I was being valued for my mind instead of defined by my legal status. These people didn't care about my conviction—they cared about my theories, my insights, my ability to think about complex problems in new ways. It reminded me that I was still a person with something to contribute.

And when I'd log off and return to the silence of my trailer, I'd think about Angie. Her laugh. The way she teased me when I got too serious. I'd remember the way she used to nudge me during movies when she could tell I was zoning out. How she called me "Trouble" like it was both a warning and a term of endearment.

Angie had seen something in me worth loving, even knowing the worst thing the world believed about me. That knowledge became a lifeline during the darkest moments—proof that I was still capable of inspiring affection, still worthy of someone's care and attention.

She wasn't the one. But she was someone. A real someone.

And in a life where most people saw me as a category rather than a person, being someone's "real someone" felt like everything.

And she helped me remember I wasn't done yet.

Not by a long shot.

Waiting in Exile

Because if I could make one person see past the label to the man underneath, maybe I could do it again. Maybe my story wasn't over. Maybe this book, these theories, this voice I was finding in the darkness—maybe all of it was just the beginning of becoming human again.

Chapter Seventeen: The Fire Still Burns

Sometimes the only way to reclaim your humanity is to fight for it with your fists. Not because violence is the answer, but because some people only understand the language of force. When words fail and dignity isn't enough, sometimes you have to remind the world—and yourself—that you're still a man who won't be broken.

Even if the fighting never really ends.

There's this thing that happens when your past precedes you into every room. You walk in, and people don't see your face, or your clothes, or even your body language. They see the headline. The registry. The label. News travels fast in my grungy little trailer park. People have already decided who you are before you get the chance to say hello.

By this point in my life, I could read a room within thirty seconds of walking into it. I could tell who had Googled me, who had heard whispers, who was just waiting for an excuse to make me the entertainment for the evening. I'd developed survival instincts I never knew I needed.

That's the kind of night it was when I found myself sitting on someone's deck, half-drunk on stale beer and playing Euchre with a table full of strangers who knew of me, but didn't know me at all.

I shouldn't have been drinking. I knew better. But sobriety is harder to maintain when you're trying to fit in with people who use alcohol as social lubrication. Sometimes you make bad choices because the alternative is sitting alone in your trailer, staring at the walls.

I'd been trying to normalize. That's what they say in therapy, right? Reintegration. Routine. Just live your life. Like that's easy. Like the world forgets.

It doesn't.

Not when you're branded.

The therapists make it sound so simple: "Engage in normal social activities. Build healthy relationships. Participate in your community." They never explain how to do that when your community sees you as a predator first and a person second.

The guy was big—tall, broad-shouldered, probably 6'3" and pushing 250. He had that kind of arrogance that fills up a room before he even says anything. I didn't know him. He didn't know me. But he knew something. Something he thought gave him power.

He had that look—the one I'd learned to recognize immediately. The gleam in his eye that said he'd been waiting all night for this moment. He'd probably been told about me before I even walked in, probably been planning this confrontation since he heard I was coming.

"Hey," he said, slurring his words, loud enough for everyone to hear. "Ain't you that child molester?"

The table went dead silent. Not the comfortable silence of people concentrating on cards, but the electric silence of people watching a car accident happen in slow motion. Everyone knew what was coming next.

I didn't flinch. Not at first. I gave him a warning look, the kind you give a man before you knock his teeth out.

"Don't call me that again," I said, calmly.

I'd learned to keep my voice level during these confrontations. Getting emotional only gives them more ammunition. The calmer you stay, the crazier they look when they keep pushing.

He smirked. Took a swig from his beer. The people at the table went quiet.

That smirk told me everything I needed to know. He wasn't just drunk—he was hunting. Looking for a reaction, for a reason to escalate. Some people get off on humiliating others, especially when they think they have moral justification.

A few hands later, he said it again. "Can't believe we're playin' cards with a damn chomo."

I stood up this time. "Last warning."

Standing was calculated. It showed I was serious without being overtly threatening. It gave him a chance to back down, to save face, to end this before it got ugly. Most smart bullies take the out.

He laughed. "What? You gonna cry, chomo?"

That laugh was his mistake. It told everyone in the room that he wasn't going to stop, that he was going to keep pushing until something broke. And since I was the only thing in the room that could break, that meant me.

I stood tall, looked him dead in the eyes, and said, "Let's go. Outside. Right now."

I'd learned that if a fight is inevitable, you control when and where it happens. Outside meant fewer people got hurt. It meant property damage was minimal. It meant witnesses but not chaos.

Everyone went quiet. There's a certain kind of silence that settles in a crowd when something real is about to happen.

You could feel the tension shift. This wasn't entertainment anymore—this was serious. People were calculating whether they should intervene, whether they should call someone, whether they wanted to watch what was about to happen. "No, you guys!" Terra yelled. It was her party, her front yard. But it was too late.

We stepped out onto the cracked concrete slab that passed for a driveway. The air was cold, sharp with tension. He took off his coat, flexed like he was getting ready to put on a show.

He was still performing, still playing to an audience. That told me he'd never been in a real fight—just bar room scuffles where someone always broke it up before anyone got seriously hurt. This was going to be different.

"Go ahead," I said. "Take the first swing. I'm not gonna start it. But I will finish it." I stuck out my chin...

I needed him to swing first. Not for legal reasons—I was past caring about legal consequences. But for my own conscience. I wasn't going to be the aggressor. I was going to be the man who defended himself when defending himself became the only option left.

He didn't hesitate. He threw a haymaker right at my jaw. Landed, too. My head snapped sideways, stars flashed in my vision. But I stayed standing.

That was his mistake.

The punch hurt, but it also freed me. Now I didn't have to hold back. Now I didn't have to be the bigger man. Now I could unleash every ounce of rage I'd been carrying for years—every humiliation, every lost job, every destroyed relationship.

Gregory Paul

I lunged forward, head down, shoulders tight, and drove into his ribs like a battering ram. We both hit the ground hard. He tried to roll, to throw punches, but I had already mounted him and started raining blows down like a thunderstorm.

This wasn't boxing. This wasn't sport. This was years of systematic dehumanization finding its outlet in my fists connecting with his face. Every punch was for every time someone had called me a monster. Every impact was for every door that had been slammed in my face.

I don't know how many times I hit him—ten, twelve, maybe more. All I remember is the blood. His nose, his mouth, his eye swelling shut.

At some point, the rage transformed into something colder, more focused. I wasn't angry anymore—I was working. Each punch was deliberate, calculated, designed to send a message that would echo far beyond this driveway.

Someone screamed. A few people rushed out and pulled me off him. He staggered up, dazed and bleeding, and stumbled away into the night like a deer that just learned what a hunter looks like.

When they pulled me off, I didn't resist. The job was done. The message was sent. He'd think twice before calling someone else that word, and everyone who watched would remember what happened when you pushed Gregory Paul too far.

The crowd erupted! Applause. Shouts. One guy clapped me on the back and said, "Jesus, Greg, I've never seen anything like that in my life."

The applause felt hollow. These same people had been content to watch me get humiliated until I fought back. Now they wanted to celebrate the violence they'd been too cowardly to prevent. Their approval meant nothing.

My knuckles were busted open, raw and bleeding, but I felt calm. Not proud. Not vindicated. Just... still.

The stillness was the strangest part. For the first time in years, the constant background noise of rage and humiliation had gone quiet. I'd finally done something about it, and the relief was almost overwhelming.

I walked back inside, sat down at the table, and picked up my cards. Nobody said a word. The silence wasn't tense anymore. It was reverent.

That reverent silence told me everything about how these people really saw me. They respected violence more than they respected humanity. They'd needed to see me hurt someone before they could see me as a person.

That fight wasn't just about the insult. It was about everything. Every job I lost. Every phone call that ended in hate. Every look of disgust from people who had no idea what really happened. That fight was the pressure valve blowing wide open.

But it didn't fix anything.

Violence never fixes anything—it just temporarily redistributes the pain. I'd hurt him to make myself feel better, but the registry was still there. The conviction was still there. The systematic exclusion was still there. All I'd done was prove I could still bleed like everyone else.

The next morning, I woke up sore as hell. My knuckles were swollen, and my head throbbed like someone had dropped a cinder block on it. But the pain reminded me I was still alive.

The physical pain was almost welcome. It was honest, immediate, fixable. Unlike the psychological pain I carried everywhere, these injuries would heal. My knuckles would stop hurting. My head would stop throbbing. But I'd still be Gregory Paul the sex offender tomorrow.

I still had something to prove.

The fight had proven I could defend myself, but it hadn't proven I was innocent. It hadn't proven I deserved compassion. It had just proven I was dangerous when cornered—which was exactly what everyone already believed about me.

Later that day, I found myself scrolling through old pictures of Jenna. She couldn't have been more than seven in the one that stopped me cold. She was wearing this oversized hoodie and standing in front of my old apartment, holding a pumpkin we carved together. Her grin was pure sunlight.

Looking at that picture felt like being punched all over again. Here I was, having just beaten a man bloody in a driveway, staring at the face of the child I'd lost because the world believed I was capable of hurting children. The irony was suffocating.

That image shattered me.

I flashed back to her bedroom in Clinton Township. I had set up a dome tent in the corner, filled it with blankets, pillows, her favorite stuffed animals. The walls were decorated with Blue's Clues, Toy Story, and The Lion King. We'd lie there together, staring up at the stars I'd stuck to the ceiling, making up stories about which ones might be real. She used to call it our spaceship. And I'd call her my co-pilot.

Waiting in Exile

Those memories felt like they belonged to someone else—a different Gregory who lived in a different world where fathers could love their daughters without suspicion, where bedtime stories weren't evidence of predatory behavior, where being gentle with a child was seen as natural instead of sinister.

Those nights felt like another life.

Because they were another life. The Greg who set up that tent and told those stories was a man who believed in fairness, who thought the truth mattered, who assumed the system was designed to protect the innocent. That man died the day they raided my apartment.

Back at Terra's that night, nobody talked about what happened. But the story spread. It always does. The whispers softened. The taunts disappeared. And for once, people looked at me like I was a man again—not a monster.

But I knew the truth.

The respect I'd earned through violence was temporary and conditional. It would last until the next drunk asshole decided to test me, until the next person who'd never been punched in the face decided to see what I was made of. I'd won a battle, not a war.

It was only a matter of time before someone else took his place. Another drunk. Another big mouth. Another fight I couldn't win with fists.

Because the real enemy wasn't drunk assholes in trailer parks. The real enemy was a system that turned me into a target, that painted a bullseye on my back and then acted surprised when people took shots at me. You can't fight a system with your fists.

That's when I knew the war I was fighting wasn't out there anymore.

It was inside.

The external battles—the confrontations, the humiliations, the rejections—were just symptoms. The real war was the one happening in my head, between the man I used to be and the man the world insisted I was. Between my knowledge of my innocence and everyone else's certainty of my guilt.

And that battle was far from over.

But at least now I knew where the real fighting needed to happen. Not in the yard with drunk strangers, but in the space between who I'd been and who I was becoming. The question was whether I could win a war against myself. The fight had proven I could defend myself, but it hadn't proven I was innocent. It hadn't proven I deserved compassion. It had just proven I was dangerous when cornered—which was exactly what everyone already believed about me.

Later that day, I found myself scrolling through old pictures of Jenna. She couldn't have been more than seven in the one that stopped me cold. She was wearing this oversized hoodie and standing in front of my old apartment, holding a pumpkin we carved together. Her grin was pure sunlight.

Looking at that picture felt like being punched all over again. Here I was, having just beaten a man bloody in a driveway, staring at the face of the child I'd lost because the world believed I was capable of hurting children. The irony was suffocating.

That image shattered me.

Waiting in Exile

I flashed back to her bedroom in Clinton Township. I had set up a dome tent in the corner, filled it with blankets, pillows, her favorite stuffed animals. The walls were decorated with Blue's Clues, Toy Story, and The Lion King. We'd lie there together, staring up at the stars I'd stuck to the ceiling, making up stories about which ones might be real. She used to call it our spaceship. And I'd call her my co-pilot.

Those memories felt like they belonged to someone else—a different Gregory who lived in a different world where fathers could love their daughters without suspicion, where bedtime stories weren't evidence of predatory behavior, where being gentle with a child was seen as natural instead of sinister.

Those nights felt like another life.

Because they were another life. The Gregory who set up that tent and told those stories was a man who believed in fairness, who thought the truth mattered, who assumed the system was designed to protect the innocent. That man died the day they raided my apartment.

Back at the garage that night, nobody talked about what happened. But the story spread. It always does. The whispers softened. The taunts disappeared. And for once, people looked at me like I was a man again—not a monster.

The respect I'd earned through violence was temporary and conditional. It would last until the next drunk asshole decided to test me, until the next person who'd never been punched in the face decided to see what I was made of. I'd won a battle, not a war.

But I knew the truth.

Gregory Paul

It was only a matter of time before someone else took his place. Another drunk. Another big mouth. Another fight I couldn't win with fists.

Because the real enemy wasn't drunk assholes in garages. The real enemy was a system that turned me into a target, that painted a bullseye on my back and then acted surprised when people took shots at me. You can't fight a system with your fists.

That's when I knew the war I was fighting wasn't out there anymore.

It was inside.

The external battles—the confrontations, the humiliations, the rejections—were just symptoms. The real war was the one happening in my head, between the man I used to be and the man the world insisted I was. Between my knowledge of my innocence and everyone else's certainty of my guilt.

And that battle was far from over.

But at least now I knew where the real fighting needed to happen. Not in driveways with drunk strangers, but in the space between who I'd been and who I was becoming. The question was whether I could win a war against myself.

Chapter Eighteen: Forged in Fire

Sometimes the only way forward is through complete destruction. Not the dramatic kind that makes headlines, but the slow-motion collapse that forces you to rebuild from nothing. When every external structure in your life crumbles, you're left with a choice: disappear entirely or discover what you're actually made of underneath all the wreckage.

The answer isn't always what you expect.

There was a long stretch of time when hope felt like a joke—a word other people got to use. After jail, probation, failed jobs, and relationships turned sour, I found myself walking into places like a ghost, hoping someone might look past the scarlet letter I wore. Every time I filled out a job application, I could feel the weight of my past pressing down on the page, as if my own handwriting screamed unemployable.

The registry had turned every job application into an act of futility. I'd fill them out knowing the background check would kill any chance I had, but I kept doing it anyway. Because the alternative was giving up completely, and I wasn't ready for that yet.

But I kept trying. I put in applications everywhere—restaurants, warehouses, hardware stores, even gas stations. Anything. But nothing ever came of it. I wasn't even getting callbacks. Just silence. Or worse—the awkward phone calls where someone would finally say, "We appreciate your interest, but we've decided to go in another direction." That direction was never toward someone like me.

Each rejection felt like confirmation that I'd been permanently exiled from the world of normal employment. Not because I couldn't do the work, not because I wasn't qualified, but because a computer database said I was dangerous. My skills didn't matter. My work ethic didn't matter. Only the label mattered.

Eventually, it wasn't just about money. It was about survival. I had to find something to keep me tethered to this world. I was slipping. Again. The second nervous breakdown wasn't just in my rearview mirror—it was waving me back in like a damn traffic cop.

I could feel myself disappearing again, becoming more ghost than man. When you can't work, can't contribute, can't prove your worth to society, you start to question whether you have any worth at all. The breakdown wasn't coming—it was already here, just taking its time finishing the job.

That's when my dad offered me something that I didn't even recognize at first: a lifeline.

"Come work in the shop with me," he said. "I could use the help."

It wasn't charity, though it could have felt like it. It was my father seeing his son drowning and throwing him the only rope he had. He was offering me something no one else would: the chance to be useful again.

Downriver Welding in Detroit wasn't a big operation. It was a retirement project, a hobby really. A place for my father to keep busy, do a few small jobs, and stay out of the house. But when I showed up and started working with him, something shifted.

Walking into that shop felt like stepping into a parallel universe where my conviction didn't exist. Here, I was just another set of hands, another mind working on problems that needed solving. The metal didn't care about my past. The machines didn't judge me.

We were building again. Creating. Not just fabricating metal, but constructing something with purpose. Little by little, we turned his side project into a full-fledged business. We got clients. Contracts. People started to know the name. I was good at it. I had always been mechanically inclined, and now, I finally had a chance to prove I was more than a label on a database.

For the first time since my conviction, I was being judged by the quality of my work instead of the content of my criminal record. Customers didn't know who I was—they only knew whether their welding job was done right. And it always was.

And for a while, things were good. Really good.

Those were the closest I'd come to feeling normal since the raid. Getting up in the morning with a purpose, solving problems with my hands and my brain, earning money through honest work—it felt like I was slowly becoming human again.

Then 2017 happened.

I should have known it couldn't last. The registry doesn't let you escape that easily. If the system can't destroy you socially, it'll find another way.

I remember the accident vividly. I had just left Planet Fitness after a short workout and was stopped at a light when it happened. The guy hit me from behind doing 50. I never saw him coming. It felt like a cannonball hit the back of my car. My spine bent like a piece of wire under pressure, and the pain that shot through me wasn't just physical—it was a warning. A new chapter was about to begin, and it wasn't going to be a good one.

The irony wasn't lost on me. Just when I'd found something good, something that made me feel valuable again, fate decided to remind me that I wasn't allowed to have nice things. The accident felt like the universe putting me back in my place.

After that, I was never the same. Three spinal fusion surgeries later, I still can't do the physical labor I once could. Welding is a hands-on trade. You can't do it from a chair with a heating pad and pain meds. I was out. My body had betrayed me.

Losing the ability to weld felt like losing my last connection to usefulness. The registry had already taken my career in restaurants, and now this accident had taken my ability to work with my hands. I was running out of ways to prove I was worth keeping around.

But my mind? That was still on fire.

Physical disability forced me to discover intellectual capability I didn't know I had. When your body fails you, you either give up or you find out what else you're capable of. I chose to find out.

I had always been curious—philosophically inclined, a late-blooming nerd. Theoretical physics became more than a fascination; it became a calling. I started reading papers, watching lectures, challenging my brain in ways I never had before. I discovered a truth about myself: my disability had made me more intellectually alive than ever before.

This wasn't compensation for physical loss—this was discovery of intellectual capacity that had been dormant my whole life. Pain forced me to explore parts of my mind I'd never accessed. It was like finding a secret room in a house you'd lived in for forty years.

Writing became my therapy. My discipline. My sword.

If I couldn't build with metal anymore, I'd build with words. If I couldn't shape steel, I'd shape ideas. If the world wouldn't let me contribute physically, I'd contribute intellectually. Writing became my defiance against a system that wanted me to disappear.

I was diagnosed with ADHD and bipolar II. For the first time in my life, things started making sense. The chaos, the impulsivity, the waves of emotion and obsession—they all had names now. And with those names came treatment. I started therapy. Got on the right meds. My mind, once a cage of chaos, began to quiet.

The diagnoses were liberating in the strangest way. Suddenly, my whole life made sense—the restaurant failures, the relationship disasters, the inability to stay on track. It wasn't character flaws or moral failures. It was brain chemistry. And brain chemistry could be treated.

That's when I began working on the Awareness Field theory. A dissertation, really. An exploration of consciousness, causality, and the structure of reality. I had no formal degree, but I didn't need one to ask the questions. Why are we here? What observes the observer? Is awareness fundamental? Why else would a wave become a particle only when being watched?

The theory became my obsession in the best possible way. Here was something that required everything I had—intellectual rigor, creative thinking, sustained focus—and nobody could take it away from me. The registry couldn't revoke my ability to think.

It was like building something again. Like welding, but for the soul.

The comparison wasn't accidental. Both welding and theoretical physics require you to take separate elements and fuse them into something stronger than the sum of their parts. I was applying the same creative process to quantum mechanics that I'd once applied to metal.

In those early writing sessions, I would sit at my desk for hours, hammering out ideas, rewriting concepts, losing myself in the flow. One day, I wrote for 14 hours straight without realizing it. I hadn't felt that kind of momentum since the early days in the shop with my dad. I couldn't lift steel anymore, but I could lift ideas. Bend them. Shape them. Forge them.

Those marathon writing sessions were like meditation, prayer, and rebellion all at once. For 14 hours, I wasn't Gregory the sex offender. I was Gregory Paul the thinker, the questioner, the man trying to understand consciousness itself. The registry couldn't touch me there.

Every once in a while, I'd look at the scars on my back and remind myself: this pain gave birth to something.

The scars became proof that destruction can lead to creation, that sometimes you have to lose everything before you can discover what you're actually capable of building.

My father and I—well, we started to butt heads. He had a worker's mentality. I had business acumen. That tension simmered just beneath the surface. Arguments sparked over things like invoices, materials, or how to approach a job. It wasn't just about welding—it was about control. About purpose. About feeling like I still had a place in the world.

The tension with my father was really about two different philosophies of survival. He believed in keeping your head down and doing honest work. I believed in thinking strategically, building something bigger. Both approaches had merit, but they were incompatible in the same small shop.

Eventually, it became clear that I couldn't keep doing this forever. My back couldn't handle it. My spirit couldn't handle it. I needed something of my own. Something sustainable. And that's when I realized that the only real currency I had left—was words.

Words were the one thing the system couldn't regulate, couldn't license, couldn't deny me access to. Nobody could run a background check on my ability to think or prevent me from putting sentences together. Language was my last remaining freedom.

I put myself in therapy not just to survive, but to grow. I didn't want to spend the rest of my life defined by what I was. I wanted to be known for what I am. A writer. A thinker. A man trying to be more.

Therapy wasn't about fixing what was broken—it was about building something new from the pieces that remained. I wasn't trying to get back to who I used to be. I was trying to become someone I'd never been before.

I started to realize that maybe, just maybe, this book—this collection of pain and reflection and raw, unfiltered truth—could be something. Maybe it could find others like me. Maybe it could shake something loose in the world.

The book became my way of turning suffering into purpose. If I had to carry this pain, I could at least use it to help others who were carrying the same burden. If I had to be exiled, I could at least map the territory for those who came after me.

I began to believe again.

Not in the system, not in justice, not in fairness—but in the possibility that a man could rebuild himself from nothing. That intelligence and determination could overcome systematic exclusion. That words could be weapons against a world that wanted you to disappear.

The work was far from over, but I was finally climbing—not just out of a hole, but toward something higher. And the burn in my back? It reminded me every day that I had earned this climb.

Every step up that mountain hurt, but the pain was proof that I was moving. The scars were evidence that I'd survived what was meant to destroy me. The burn was fuel for the fire that drove me forward.

But now the fire was controlled, directed, purposeful. I wasn't being consumed by the flames anymore—I was using them to light the way forward for anyone else lost in the darkness.

Chapter Nineteen: Triggered

There's a moment in every man's life when he learns the difference between fighting and winning. Sometimes you discover that the real battle was never about proving you could take a punch or throw one—it was about proving you didn't have to. Sometimes you have to lose a fight to win the war for your own soul.

And sometimes, getting your ass kicked is exactly what saves your life.

There's a moment in every man's life when he has to decide who he's going to be. Not who he was, not who the world says he is, but who he becomes when the pressure cracks and the moment explodes. Sometimes that moment comes with a clear choice. Sometimes it comes with someone else's fist flying at your face. And sometimes, you find out the man you are isn't the man you thought you were.

By this point in my journey, I'd been seeing Karen for months. The therapy was helping—slowly rewiring the parts of my brain that had learned to expect violence, preparing me for confrontation, treating every social situation like a potential battlefield. But knowing something intellectually and living it in the moment are two completely different things.

It happened one summer Friday night. We were at a buddy's place in the trailer park, just a few of us playing Euchre, drinking cheap beer, enjoying the warmth. One of those rare nights when things almost felt normal. The kind of normal you learn not to trust. And all it took to shatter it was a word.

I'd been doing so well. Staying sober most days, writing regularly, actually believing Karen when she said I was more than my label. And then this night happened, reminding me how fragile that progress really was.

He was new. Big black guy. Broad shoulders, about 6 foot 3. Probably ex-football. I hadn't seen him before, but I knew the type. Something in his posture told me he'd already made up his mind about me. I'd developed a radar for that—sensing when someone in the room was stewing on something they thought they needed to say. He was standing by the fridge, red Solo cup in hand, watching me. Studying me like I was a threat or a test.

That radar had become second nature by now—a survival skill I'd developed through dozens of these confrontations. I could feel the tension building, could see him working up to it. Part of me wanted to leave right then. The smarter part. But pride kept me in that chair.

Then he said it. Loud and clear, like a challenge thrown in the dirt.

"You know this guy's a chomo, right?"

Everything stopped. You could feel the oxygen leave the trailer. Cards hit the table. Conversations froze mid-sentence. Every set of eyes turned toward me.

I looked up slow. "Say that again?"

He didn't blink. "I said you're a chomo. What, you gonna deny it?"

His grin made my stomach twist. This wasn't about safety. It was a performance. A dominance display. He was going to be the hero who exposed the monster. All he needed was a stage.

And I was about to give him exactly what he wanted—proof that I was everything they said I was.

Waiting in Exile

I tried to control it. One... two... three. I'd learned that counting trick in therapy. Breathe. Respond, don't react. But that trick was starting to rot.

Karen's voice was in my head: "You don't have to prove anything to anyone." But in that moment, surrounded by watching eyes and judgment, I couldn't hear her clearly enough.

"You don't know me," I said. "And you don't want to do this."

He turned to the crowd. "Heard it from three people. I got nieces two trailers down. He doesn't belong here."

"He doesn't belong here." That phrase hit harder than any slur. This was about territory, about deciding I didn't deserve to exist in their community, their space, their world.

"That's strike one," I said, standing up.

He stepped closer. "Go ahead. Hit me, chomo."

Strike two.

Each repetition of that word stripped away another layer of the control I'd been building in therapy. Each use was designed to provoke exactly this response—to turn me into the violent offender they already believed I was.

"Last chance," I said, louder now.

He drew it out this time. "CHO-MO."

Strike three.

I walked out the front door and into the humid night, heart hammering. I wasn't even mad—I was burning. Walked around to the side yard where it was darker, quieter. Waited.

Walking outside was supposed to be the smart move—removing bystanders, controlling the environment. But really, I was just giving us privacy to do something I'd regret. Karen would ask me later why I didn't just keep walking. I still don't have a good answer.

He followed like I knew he would. Chest out. Shoulders back. You'd think he was stepping into a ring.

I turned and faced him.

"Go ahead," I said, pointing to my chin. "You swing first. I'm not starting this."

That distinction mattered to me—being the defender, not the aggressor. Like it would somehow make the violence more justified, more righteous. Like there was a moral difference between throwing the first punch and taking it. There wasn't.

He didn't hesitate. That fist came fast. Cracked me right in the jaw. And just like that—I was gone.

The fight was fast. Dirty. Honest in the way only violence can be. We wrestled, punched, slammed into the fence. But he had the upper hand from the start. I was seeing stars and trying to stay upright. Eventually, I went down. He landed a few more. My face was wet with blood and gravel.

All those years of rage, all that accumulated injustice, all the systematic humiliation—none of it made me a better fighter. It just made me angrier while I was losing. The movies lie about righteous fury giving you superhuman strength. In reality, anger just makes you sloppy.

He stood over me and spat. Walked off without a word.

No victory. No redemption. Just silence.

And in that silence, lying there tasting blood and dirt, something shifted. The rage that had been burning for years suddenly felt cold, used up, pointless. I'd finally done what I'd been wanting to do—fought back—and it had solved exactly nothing.

Someone helped me up. Someone else mumbled, "Let's call it even." I barely heard them.

"Call it even." Like violence could balance some cosmic ledger, like my blood on the ground somehow settled accounts. Nothing was even. Nothing was settled. I'd just given them exactly what they expected—a violent offender proving he was violent.

I stumbled home. My head throbbing. Jaw swollen. Hands torn up. I sat on the porch and stared into the darkness, barely breathing. Then I wept.

I cried not because I lost. I cried because I still thought I needed to fight in the first place. I cried because I gave him exactly what he wanted. I became the monster they already believed I was.

The tears weren't about physical pain—they were about the realization that I'd betrayed myself. All the work with Karen, all the writing, all the slow progress toward becoming something better than what they said I was—I'd thrown it all away for what? For pride? For the temporary satisfaction of swinging back? For proving I could bleed?

I cried because I had been trying so hard—to walk straight, to stay quiet, to live small. And none of it mattered. One guy with a big mouth and a bigger fist undid all of it.

And the truth? Part of me had been waiting for that moment. Waiting for a reason to let the rage out. And it felt so good in those seconds when the fists were flying. But it wasn't justice. It was just more pain stacked on top of the mountain I already carried.

That recognition was the hardest part—admitting that I'd wanted the fight, that some part of me had been looking for an excuse to unleash years of accumulated fury. The system hadn't just victimized me. It had changed me into someone who craved violence as release.

Later that week, I sat in Karen's office. Still sore. Still stiff. My right eye still tinged purple.

She didn't comment on the bruises at first. Just let the silence do the work.

Eventually she asked, "What happened?"

"Got in a fight," I said. "Tried to walk away. Gave him the first shot. But yeah... I got my ass kicked."

Saying it out loud made it real in a way it hadn't been before. Not just that I'd lost, but that I'd participated. That I'd chosen violence even knowing it would solve nothing.

Karen was quiet, then said, "Why did you stay?"

"Because if I walked away, I'd hate myself more than if I got beat down. Because I've been swallowing this shit for years. And I guess I thought I needed to remind the world—and myself—that I could still bleed and swing."

It was the truth, even if it made me look weak. I'd stayed because walking away felt like surrender, like admitting they were right about me being less than human. Fighting back felt like reclaiming something. But I'd been wrong.

She nodded slowly. "And now?"

"Now I feel stupid. I feel tired."

She didn't flinch. "You've earned the right to be tired. But violence isn't where your power lives. That's where their fear of you lives. Not your strength."

Waiting in Exile

That distinction cut through everything. She was right. Every time I fought, I was confirming their fears, giving them evidence that I was dangerous. My real power—the thing that actually threatened their narrative—was my ability to remain human despite everything they'd done to dehumanize me.

That cut deeper than any punch.

I told her I didn't want to be feared anymore. I wanted peace. I wanted to be left the fuck alone.

Karen looked at me and said, "Then stop proving them right. Stop living in the mold they cast for you. Start building your own."

Building my own. Not fighting against theirs, not proving anything to anyone, just building something new from scratch. That concept was so simple it felt revolutionary.

I left her office and sat in my car for thirty minutes. I didn't turn the ignition. I just sat there, fingers wrapped around the steering wheel, realizing how far I'd drifted from the man I wanted to be. From the man I used to be. From the man I could still become—if I did something different.

The man who'd set up a tent in Jenna's bedroom wouldn't have gotten into that fight. The man who'd spent hours holding her while she slept wouldn't have needed to prove he could bleed and swing. Somewhere between being that father and becoming this exile, I'd lost track of who I really was.

That night on the porch, I started writing again. Pulled out the notebook I'd stuffed in a drawer months ago. The one I kept telling myself I'd get back to. My hands still ached, but they worked. I wrote about the fight. About the porch. About what it feels like to be hated without context, feared without cause.

And it poured out of me.

I wrote until the sun came up.

The words came faster than they had in months, like the fight had broken open some dam I'd built against my own truth. For hours, I wrote about rage and loss and systematic dehumanization, about loving a daughter I couldn't see and surviving in a world that wanted me dead.

Pages turned. Pen scratched. And for the first time since the label had been seared into my skin, I didn't feel powerless. I felt clear.

That's the difference between pain and clarity. One drowns you. The other wakes you up.

Pain just accumulates, weighing you down until you can't move. Clarity cuts through the weight, showing you exactly what you're carrying and why. That night, I finally saw clearly: violence would never free me. Only truth could do that.

I didn't write because I was healed. I wrote because I was bleeding and I didn't want to make anyone else bleed with me. I wrote because violence had taken enough from me. I wasn't going to give it anything else.

I began to realize that the real fight was never with him. It wasn't even with the system.

The real fight was with the part of me that still believed I had to prove I existed through pain. That part of me—the wounded animal who thought his worth was tied to how many punches he could take or throw—that's the part that had to die.

That version of me had been created by systematic abuse, forged in the crucible of false conviction and permanent exile. He'd served his purpose—keeping me alive when survival meant being harder, meaner, more dangerous than they expected. But he couldn't take me any further.

And that's exactly what I buried on that porch.

That version of me—the one that bled, fought, exploded, defended with fists instead of words—he served his purpose. He kept me alive through the worst of it. But he couldn't take me any further.

If I was going to survive the long haul, I had to evolve.

Evolution meant choosing words over fists, truth over violence, writing over fighting. It meant accepting that losing a physical fight could mean winning the war for my humanity.

So I picked up the pen.

Let them call me soft. Let them call me broken. Let them call me whatever helps them sleep at night.

I know who I am.

I am Jenna's father, even though she can't see that right now. I am a writer, even though the world only sees my conviction. I am a man who chose to be beaten rather than become a monster. And that choice—that moment of losing—might be the most important victory of my life.

I am not the man who needs to swing.

I am the man who tells the truth.

And if the truth makes people uncomfortable, good.

Because this time, I'm not the one bleeding.

They are.

The system bleeds when you refuse to become what it says you are. Society bleeds when you show them the human cost of their comfortable assumptions. The narrative bleeds

Gregory Paul

when you write your own story instead of living the one they wrote for you.

That night on the porch, I didn't win a fight. But I won something more important: I won myself back.

And no amount of violence could ever give me that.

Chapter Twenty: The Long Climb

Recovery isn't a straight line from broken to whole. It's a zigzag path up a mountain where every step forward might be followed by two steps back, where the summit keeps disappearing behind clouds, where you're never quite sure if you're climbing toward something better or just exhausting yourself for nothing.

But you keep climbing anyway, because the alternative is staying in the valley where nothing grows.

By the time I rolled into therapy that next scheduled day, I was still carrying the heat of that last fight in my fists. My knuckles had healed, but something deeper hadn't. There was a storm inside me, the kind that doesn't just pass. It roots itself in your bones. The kind you carry long after the bruises fade.

I'd reached the point where violence felt normal, where my first instinct in any confrontation was to calculate whether I could win the fight. That wasn't who I'd been before the conviction, and it scared me more than any threat from the outside world.

Karen, my therapist, was not what I expected. Older woman, gray streaks in her hair, dressed like she read minds for a living. She looked me up and down—not with judgment, but with curiosity. Like she'd seen every kind of man walk through that door and knew which ones were full of it. I told myself I wasn't going to play games. I would be honest—or at least, as honest as I could be.

There was something about Karen's complete lack of shock or fear that told me she'd worked with people carrying real darkness before. She wasn't impressed by my conviction or intimidated by my history. To her, I was just another human being trying to figure out how to live with himself.

"Why are you here, Greg?" she asked, folding her hands across her lap.

I looked at the floor, then up again. "Because everyone else thinks I'm a monster. And I need to figure out if they're right."

It was the most honest thing I'd said to another human being in years. Not "I need help" or "I want to feel better," but the raw admission that I was losing the ability to distinguish between who I was and who the world said I was.

That was the first time I admitted it out loud—the doubt that crept in late at night after the world quieted. Was I the thing they made me out to be? Not in action, but in nature? Could enough repetition, enough punishment, enough humiliation, turn a man into what he swore he wasn't?

The question terrified me because I could feel myself changing. The man who'd thrown those punches in the trailer park wasn't the same man who'd once set up a tent in Jenna's bedroom. But which one was the real me? The gentle father or the violent exile?

I started seeing Karen every week. Sometimes twice. Slowly, the tension in my shoulders started to ease. I wasn't fixed. I wasn't healed. But I was seen. And that mattered more than I could admit.

Being seen without judgment felt like a miracle. For an hour at a time, I could exist in a space where my conviction wasn't the most important thing about me. Karen saw my pain, my confusion, my struggle to remain human—and she didn't flinch.

One day, after a particularly heavy session, Karen leaned in and said, "You're stronger than 99% of the people I see. And not because of what you've done—but because you're still standing after what's been done to you."

That distinction—between what I'd done and what had been done to me—felt revolutionary. Most of the world conflated the two, assuming that anyone who'd been through the system deserved whatever happened to them afterward. Karen understood that survival itself was an achievement.

That moment stuck. She wasn't congratulating me for surviving. She was acknowledging the cost. There's a difference.

The cost had been enormous—my relationship with Jenna, my career, my sense of self, my ability to trust others or believe in justice. But acknowledging that cost also meant acknowledging that I'd paid a price for something I wasn't, which was the first step toward reclaiming my innocence.

And in those same months, I kept writing. Writing had become a ritual, almost sacred. I'd sit at my table with a notebook and stare at the blank page like it owed me rent. The words came in waves. Sometimes a few trickles, sometimes a flood. But they always came.

Writing was therapy without a therapist, conversation without judgment, a place where I could be completely honest without worrying about how it sounded or whether someone would use it against me. The page never called me a monster. It just listened.

Late at night, I'd flash back to Jenna. I could still see her as a baby, fast asleep on my chest, her soft breath rising and falling. I'd kiss the top of her head and not move for hours, just so I wouldn't disturb her. That memory was both armor and anguish. It reminded me of who I had been. Who I still was, buried under all the legal branding.

Those memories of Jenna became my proof of innocence—not legal proof, but emotional proof. The man who'd spent hours holding a sleeping baby, who'd worried about waking her with his movements, who'd felt such overwhelming protective love—that man wasn't capable of hurting a child.

I thought about her letter. Every word. Her anger. Her heartbreak. Her belief that I had failed her in some unforgivable, unfixable way. But I also thought about what she hadn't said—the part that still remembered me as her dad, if only in a fractured, distant way.

The fact that she'd written at all gave me hope. Anger is easier to heal than indifference. If she still cared enough to be furious with me, maybe there was still something left to save. Maybe "Daddy" wasn't completely dead to her.

It was those gaps I wrote into. I carved space for my voice. For my version of the story. Not to defend myself, but to be heard. And maybe, one day, understood.

The writing wasn't about convincing anyone of my innocence—it was about preserving my humanity. Every page was proof that I was still capable of thought, reflection, growth. That I was more than just a conviction and a registry number.

Mia was still around then. She could tell I was disappearing into myself again. One night, after dinner, she looked across the table and said, "You talk more to your paper than you do to me."

She wasn't wrong. I had found something in writing that no person could match—a mirror that didn't flinch.

Waiting in Exile

Mia's observation stung because it was true. I was emotionally safer with words on a page than with another human being. Words couldn't leave me, couldn't be turned against me, couldn't decide I was too damaged to love. But they also couldn't love me back.

I was also diving deeper into theoretical physics. The Observer Effect. The measurement problem. It was like peeling back the universe to find out if maybe—just maybe—awareness itself had a role in shaping reality. If observation changed the outcome, maybe I had been seen all wrong from the beginning. Maybe that was the real crime: being misunderstood by a world that only sees shadows.

The physics gave me a framework for understanding what had happened to me. I'd been observed incorrectly, labeled incorrectly, and that incorrect observation had collapsed my reality into something unrecognizable. But if observation could destroy, maybe it could also heal.

By spring, I had completed the first rough draft of my dissertation. It was raw. Unpolished. Riddled with tangents. But it was mine. Something no registry could take away.

The dissertation represented intellectual freedom in its purest form. No background check could prevent me from thinking about "Universal Awareness." No conviction could invalidate my theories about observation and reality. In the realm of ideas, I was free.

Still, the ankle bracelet had been gone for years, and yet it still buzzed in my mind. That phantom surveillance never really stops. You begin to monitor yourself like you're still being watched. Like Big Brother moved inside your own skull.

The psychological monitoring was more insidious than the physical device had ever been. I'd internalized the surveillance, become my own parole officer, constantly watching myself for signs of deviance that existed only in other people's fears.

But therapy was helping. Slowly. I'd still get triggered—a glance, a whisper, a news story about someone who actually had done something horrific—and I'd feel the burn of association. But I was learning how to hold my ground.

The triggers were getting easier to manage, not because they hurt less, but because I was developing tools to process them. I was learning to separate other people's crimes from my own identity, to refuse the guilt-by-association that the world tried to impose.

Karen kept saying, "Greg, you're not your label. You're your actions. Your integrity. You're your resilience."

Some days, I believed her.

On the good days, I could see myself through Karen's eyes—as a man who'd endured systematic dehumanization and somehow managed to remain human. On the bad days, all I could see was the label, what I'd lost, my conviction and the way the world looked at me.

There were moments when I'd sit outside on my porch and just breathe. Watch the stars. Think about how far I'd fallen—and how far I still had to climb. The silence was different now. Not punishment, but reflection.

The silence had transformed from something that trapped me to something that freed me. It was no longer the absence of acceptance—it was the presence of peace. Space to think, to process, to simply exist without performing for anyone.

I remembered the night Jenna and I watched Red Hot Chili Peppers videos on my computer. We'd sing together, make goofy faces, and burn our moments onto Kodak Picture CDs. We had ten or twelve of those things. Memories. Tangible ones. The law stole those from me. Raided the house and took my hard copies of joy. But they didn't steal them from my head. I only hope Jenna still remembers.

Those confiscated CDs represented more than just evidence—they were proof of our relationship, documentation of our joy, tangible reminders of who we'd been together. Taking them was like trying to erase our history, but you can't seize memories from someone's mind.

There was her room, too. Back in the Clinton Township apartment. I had put up a dome tent over her bed, decorated the walls with Blue's Clues, Toy Story, and The Lion King. I'd lay there with her for hours, watching the ceiling like it was a sky we could fly through. We'd talk about anything and everything. Those were real moments. They mattered.

The tent had been my way of creating a private universe just for us, a place where we could escape reality and imagine ourselves anywhere. Now those memories felt like evidence of innocence—what predator creates safe spaces for children to dream?

And there were the apple orchard trips with Grandma Linda. Donuts, cider, corn mazes, and haystacks. The smell of autumn and laughter in the air. For those hours, everything was normal. Everything was good.

Those autumn afternoons represented normal family life—three generations sharing simple pleasures, Jenna learning about traditions, me being just another dad helping his daughter pick apples. The conviction had stolen our future, but it couldn't steal the sweetness of those perfect days.

But depression is a silent killer. And I had sunk more than once.

The depression wasn't sadness—it was emptiness. A complete inability to imagine that tomorrow might be different from today, that I might ever be anything other than what the conviction had made me.

There was a time when I spent weeks sleeping 18 hours a day. Getting up only for cigarettes, bathroom breaks, the occasional turkey pot pie or spoonful of peanut butter. I'd sit in the dark with only the hum of the fridge to keep me company. One night, I stared at a bottle of sleeping pills. Sixty of them. And I thought, With my luck, I'd just end up brain-dead. A burden to everyone. No peace. Just another kind of exile.

The sleeping pills represented the ultimate escape from a life that felt unlivable. But even in my darkest moment, some part of me rejected that solution. I'd already been branded as someone dangerous—I wouldn't give them the satisfaction of being right about my being self-destructive too.

So I didn't do it. I repeated the phrase, "This, too, shall pass," over and over like a mantra.

It always did. Eventually.

"This too shall pass" became my anchor in the storm. Not because I believed things would get better, but because I'd learned that even the worst pain eventually changes form. Nothing stays exactly the same forever—not even hopelessness.

And that's the point. Chapter 20 wasn't a conclusion. It wasn't triumph. It was a turning point. A slow crawl out of the pit. With therapy, writing, and a stubborn belief that I still mattered—even if no one else thought I did.

Waiting in Exile

The turning point wasn't dramatic or definitive. It was the accumulation of small choices—to keep breathing, to keep writing, to keep climbing. Recovery measured in inches rather than miles, but movement nonetheless.

Karen once told me, "The human spirit is harder to kill than most people realize."

I believe that now.

The system had tried to kill my spirit systematically—through isolation, humiliation, violence, rejection. But something in me had refused to die. Call it stubbornness, call it survival instinct, call it grace—whatever it was, it had kept me alive when I didn't want to be.

I am still here.

Still climbing.

Still writing.

And as long as I'm still writing, I'm still becoming. Still discovering who I am underneath all the labels and convictions and other people's fears. Still proving that a man can survive his own destruction and build something new from the rubble.

The climb isn't over. Maybe it never will be. But every word I write is another step up the mountain, another refusal to let them bury me alive. And that's enough. For now, that's enough.

Gregory Paul

Chapter Twenty-One: A Light Through the Cracks

The end of a story like this doesn't come with resolution—it comes with recognition. Recognition that survival itself is victory. That choosing to remain human in a system designed to strip your humanity is the most radical act of defiance possible. That writing your own story when the world has already decided what your story means is how you take back your life, one word at a time.

This isn't an ending. It's a beginning disguised as an ending.

Some things never get resolved. Some wounds scab over, but they itch forever. And yet, even in the quiet corners of pain, something unexpected can happen—hope. Not loud. Not grand. But steady, like a pulse.

Hope in exile doesn't announce itself with fanfare. It arrives quietly, in the space between one breath and the next, in the moment when you realize you've made it through another day without being destroyed by it. It's not the hope of rescue—it's the hope of endurance.

There's no bow on this story. No courtroom reversal. No teary reunion at an airport. My name is still buried in the digital graveyard of registries. Jenna still hasn't called. And the public still believes headlines over heartbeats.

But something changed.

Something had to.

The change wasn't external—no laws were overturned, no public apologies were issued. The change was internal, molecular, cellular. The slow recognition that I could be destroyed by the system or shaped by it, but I couldn't be erased by it. Not completely.

It started in the smallest way. I got up one morning and didn't feel dread. That doesn't sound like much—but for someone who's spent years waking up and wishing they hadn't, it was monumental. I brewed coffee. I opened a notebook. And I wrote without crying.

That morning felt like emerging from underwater after nearly drowning. The air was the same, the world unchanged, but my lungs worked differently. For the first time in years, consciousness didn't feel like punishment. It felt like possibility.

That's what survival looks like when it isn't romantic.

Real survival isn't cinematic. It's not about dramatic confrontations or inspiring speeches. It's about waking up and choosing not to give up. It's about finding reasons to keep going when there are no good reasons left. It's about writing when your hands shake and breathing when your chest feels crushed.

I walked through hell for over a decade. A year in jail. Five years of probation. Psychological torture. Losing jobs, losing dignity, losing the right to be seen as a human being. I fought to maintain sanity when the world told me I didn't deserve it. When strangers thought they knew me. When friends walked away. When family kept their distance. When the woman I loved couldn't deal with the pressure and the whispers and the lies.

The inventory of loss reads like a catalog of systematic destruction: career, reputation, relationships, sense of self, faith in justice, belief in fairness, trust in others, trust in myself. They took everything that could be taken. But they couldn't take the part of me that observed the taking. They couldn't touch the witness.

And worst of all... when my daughter believed the noise instead of my voice.

That betrayal cut deeper than all the others combined because it was the one that mattered most. Jenna wasn't just anyone—she was my daughter, my co-pilot, my spaceship companion. If I couldn't convince her of my innocence, how could I convince myself? If she couldn't see past the conviction to the father underneath, who could?

But even so—I'm still here.

Somehow.

"Somehow" carries the weight of a thousand small choices, a thousand moments when giving up would have been easier than continuing. Somehow is the accumulation of stubborn refusal to disappear quietly. Somehow is grace disguised as stubbornness.

I've started to see cracks in the wall. Not because the system changed. Not because anyone apologized. But because I changed. Because I refused to let their narrative become my truth. I stood my ground, even when I was broken.

The cracks aren't in their wall—they're in the wall I'd built around myself. The wall of shame, of acceptance, of believing I deserved what happened to me. When that wall started cracking, light got in. Not much at first, but enough to see by.

I kept writing.

Writing became my form of resistance, my way of refusing to be silenced. Every sentence was an act of defiance against a system that wanted me to disappear quietly. Every page was proof that I was still thinking, still growing, still capable of contributing something meaningful to the world.

This book started as an act of desperation. A lifeline to anyone willing to read past the scarlet letter. I didn't write it for sympathy. I wrote it for truth. And for the ones out there who feel as alone as I did. The ones who lost their kids. The ones living in basements. The ones who only get interviews, never jobs. The ones who scream into pillows because no one wants to hear their version of the story.

This book is for the army of invisible people the registry system creates—the fathers separated from their children, the men unemployable despite their skills, the human beings reduced to database entries. They exist in every community, carrying shame that isn't theirs, living lives of quiet desperation that no one wants to acknowledge.

To them, I say: you're not alone. You're not finished. You're not broken beyond repair.

Your conviction is not your identity. Your worst moment is not your whole story. The label they've assigned you is not the truth of who you are. You are more than what happened to you, more than what you're accused of, more than the box they've put you in.

And to the ones who actually did what they were convicted of—you're not beyond redemption either. You made choices that hurt people, and that can't be undone. But you're still human beings capable of growth, change, and genuine remorse. The registry doesn't distinguish between guilt and innocence, between actual danger and manufactured fear. We're all trapped in the same system, and we all deserve the possibility of redemption.

And to my daughter—if she ever reads this—I say:

Gregory Paul

Jenna, I never stopped being your dad. Not in the courtroom. Not in jail. Not when they cuffed me. Not when you told me you needed space. Not even when your letter tore my heart to pieces. I was your father before the world called me a monster. And I'll die still being your father, no matter what they call me.

The conviction changed everything about our relationship except the fundamental truth that you are my daughter and I am your father. That bond was forged before the accusations, before the trial, before the conviction. It exists independent of legal proceedings and public opinion.

I remember you falling asleep on my chest, your hair warm against my chin. I remember singing Red Hot Chili Peppers together, making those Kodak CDs, laughing until we couldn't breathe. I remember your tent-bed with the air mattress and the glowing stars on the ceiling. I remember donuts at the orchard and Blue's Clues on the walls. I remember your voice calling me Dad before the silence took over.

These memories aren't just nostalgia—they're evidence. Evidence of who we were together, evidence of my love for you, evidence that the man they convicted wasn't the man who raised you. The legal system can seize computers and CDs, but it can't confiscate the love we shared.

I hope one day, you remember too.

I hope you remember not just the facts of our time together, but the feeling of being completely safe with me, completely loved, completely cherished. I hope you remember that the man who set up that tent, who stuck those stars to your ceiling, who held you while you slept—that man loved you more than his own life.

Waiting in Exile

And if you can remember that love, maybe you can begin to question the narrative that replaced it. Maybe you can ask yourself: what kind of monster creates safe spaces for children to dream? What kind of predator worries about waking a sleeping child? What kind of dangerous person builds tents for bedtime stories?

I didn't choose exile. But I'm learning how to survive it. To build something in spite of it. And maybe, one day, someone will read this and realize that we have to stop defining people by their worst accusation—or their worst moment.

Exile taught me things I never wanted to learn but needed to know. That resilience is a muscle that grows stronger under pressure. That isolation can lead to self-discovery. That being stripped of everything external forces you to discover what's essential. That the human spirit is more durable than anyone imagines.

Maybe someone will stop and say, "Wait a second. What really happened?"

That question—"What really happened?"—is all I've ever asked for. Not sympathy, not forgiveness for something I didn't do, just the willingness to look beyond the headlines and consider the possibility that the system got it wrong. That innocent people get caught in nets designed for the guilty.

Maybe one of them will be you.

Jenna, you have the power to ask that question about your own father. You have access to memories the court never heard, to knowledge of my character that no prosecutor presented. You know things about me that didn't make it into the official record. Trust what you remember. Trust who you knew me to be.

Until then, I'll keep going.

Moving forward doesn't require anyone else's permission or approval. It doesn't require vindication or apology. It requires only the decision to keep breathing, keep growing, keep contributing whatever you can to the world that tried to destroy you.

I'll keep researching. Keep expanding my work on the Awareness Field. Keep challenging the mainstream ideas in physics that say we're just dust and math. Because I believe awareness is fundamental. And maybe—just maybe—this whole universe is waiting to be seen correctly. Just like me.

The parallel isn't accidental—misperception at the quantum level and misperception in the legal system both distort reality. If awareness is fundamental to the universe, then being seen correctly matters on both cosmic and personal scales. If observation shapes reality, then how we observe each other shapes our collective human reality.

So this is where the book ends, but not the story.

Books end. Stories continue. The conviction that tried to end my story just changed its direction. Instead of the life I planned, I got the life I was given. Instead of the father I thought I'd be, I became the father I needed to be—one who loves from a distance, who fights for his daughter even when she can't fight for him.

Because the story is still being written. Every day I stay sober. Every day I don't quit. Every time I hit "save" on another chapter. Every time I put down the bottle and pick up the pen. Every time I help someone else see that they are more than their past.

The story continues in the choices I make each day—to remain human despite systematic dehumanization, to tell the truth despite a world that prefers simple narratives, to love my daughter despite the silence between us, to believe in redemption despite evidence that it's impossible.

The story continues in every person who reads this and recognizes their own struggle, their own exile, their own long climb back to humanity. In every family member who chooses love over fear, every employer who sees potential over conviction, every stranger who chooses curiosity over judgment.

There's no sunset here. No redemption arc wrapped in gold.

Just me.

Still here.

Still writing.

Still waiting in exile.

But exile isn't emptiness anymore. It's not punishment or abandonment. It's the space where I learned who I really am when everything external is stripped away. It's where I discovered that my value doesn't depend on other people's recognition, that my truth doesn't require their belief, that my love for my daughter doesn't need her permission.

Exile taught me that home isn't a place or a status or other people's approval. Home is the peace you make with yourself when the noise stops. Home is the voice you find when everyone else stops listening. Home is the story you tell when no one else will tell it for you.

I'm still waiting in exile. But I'm no longer waiting for rescue. I'm no longer waiting for vindication. I'm no longer waiting for the world to change its mind about me.

I'm waiting for my daughter to remember who her father really is. And until that day comes—if it ever comes—I'll be

Gregory Paul

here. Still writing. Still loving her. Still proving that a man can be destroyed by lies but not defined by them.

Still human. Still hopeful. Still her dad.

The exile continues. But so do I.

Waiting in Exile

www.ingramcontent.com/pod-product-compliance
Lightning Source LLC
Chambersburg PA
CBHW060502030426
42337CB00015B/1698